Thomas Read Wilkinson

Holiday Rambles

Thomas Read Wilkinson

Holiday Rambles

ISBN/EAN: 9783337293314

Printed in Europe, USA, Canada, Australia, Japan

Cover: Foto ©Thomas Meinert / pixelio.de

More available books at **www.hansebooks.com**

HOLIDAY RAMBLES.

BY

THOMAS READ WILKINSON.

> "Keep not standing, fixed and rooted,
>   Briskly venture,—briskly roam;
> Head and hand, where'er thou foot it,
>   And stout heart are still at home.
> In each land the sun does visit,
>   We are gay, whate'er betide;
> To give space for wandering is it
>   That the world was made so wide?"
>
> GOETHE.

MANCHESTER:
JAMES F. WILKINSON, GUTTENBERG WORKS, PENDLETON.
1881.

TO

MY FRIENDS AT HOME AND IN MANY LANDS

I DEDICATE THESE PAGES

WHICH RECALL SO MUCH OF SUNLIGHT

AND AFFECTION

THAT HAVE MADE LIFE WORTH LIVING.

PREFACE.

It is in response to the wishes of many friends that I have ventured to reprint these ephemera.

Since my return from the United States I have had many applications for copies of the two descriptive letters which I wrote on the voyage out. Their appearance in the *Manchester City News* constrained me to continue a record of my movements, and led me, without premeditation, to write the letters from America.

During the process of revision I have been pleasantly reminded of other journeyings in foreign parts, as well as of pedestrian excursions over mountain and moorland, in the days that are no more. And I have thought that it would not be an unsuitable occasion to insert one or two more of my earlier sketches, out of a rather numerous selection, as companion pictures, and to give variety.

I have not gone back beyond twenty years, although so long ago as 1844 I found myself writing accounts of travel in Scotland, and since then Ireland has on several occasions attracted me to her mountains and to her magnificent lonely rock-bound Western coast. In the few weeks of annual rest from the labour and care of business, I have had much enjoyment in tramping over the mountains of the Lake Country and of the Principality. But my chief delight has been to ramble through the length and breadth of Old England; so rich in quaint market towns, in villages and churches, in crosses, in Gothic Cathedrals, in ancient monasteries and Norman castles; in short, in innumerable memorials of a thousand years of history; attracted by the everlasting beauty of her cultivated fertile valleys and green pastures, rich in flocks and herds, or glowing with golden grain; by her hills and dales, her rivers and lakes, by her white cliffs, and by the all-encircling sea that laps her shores.

It is not, therefore, for lack of material for descriptions of our grand old country that I have not inserted in this volume an English tour, but rather because I thought my impressions of other lands might have more freshness for, and be more attractive to, many friends, who may not have become so accustomed to the pleasures of the home circuit, so to speak, as myself. The letters from Norway originally appeared in the *Manchester Examiner and Times*, and the description of the Passion Play in the *Springfield Republican*, Springfield, Mass., U.S.

I am exceedingly indebted to my friend Mr. GEORGE CROZIER, to whom I here tender my hearty thanks, for the illustrations which he has drawn to accompany the letters from Norway, visited by him in 1873.

To my brother I owe many thanks for the care he has bestowed in bringing out the volume.

T. R. WILKINSON.

The Polygon, Ardwick, Manchester,
    13th March, 1881.

A MONTH IN AMERICA.

I. LIVERPOOL TO QUEENSTOWN.

AT 1-45 p.m. on Saturday, the 11th of September, 1880, the steamship *Scythia* moved from her anchorage, on her voyage across the Atlantic. One of her passengers at least had looked forward to such a voyage for certainly more than twenty years, and (as the unexpected always happens) he had found himself, with only forty-eight hours' notice, on the way to realising a long-cherished idea. At the same moment that our good ship moved, another vast steamship, the *Baltic*, steamed out of the Mersey on the same voyage.

What magnificent works these ocean steamers are! There is no single achievement which so specially characterises the progress of modern times as the ocean steamer. It has bound together with enduring ties the continents of Europe and America, and made the mighty waste of waters truly the highway of the nations. We have on board some two hundred and seventy first-class passengers, besides the captain, officers, and crew. There is a large cargo, no doubt, in the hold. Besides this, each man will have two or three packages, each woman three or four at least. Let us say a thousand boxes or packages.

We sit down to breakfast at 8-30. We have luncheon; we dine at six. There is a congregating at night about nine for further refreshment of some sort. Fish, flesh, fowl, vegetables, fruits, drinks—we shall consume a small Smithfield or Covent Garden Market on the voyage. Then there are the vast furnaces deep down in the ship, with the incessant consumption of coal, and the ponderous but exquisitely-constructed machinery for pushing us over the three thousand miles of ocean. This is surely something we may reasonably consider as a conquest over difficulties, and an evidence at all events of material advancement. But with this, I think, has come advancement in other directions. The world of man has been brought nearer together; distinctions have been softened; the Christian idea of the strong helping the weak, the spirit of human sympathy, which received such an impetus in consequence of the Puritan emigration to the Western continent, has been carried round the earth, and steam and electricity are helping greatly to bring about

> "The parliament of peoples,
> The federation of the world."

Well, we parted from our friends truly with an undercurrent of sadness, but with pleasant mirth upon our lips. With a hearty cheer the tender slipped behind, and we were actually making for the Western World.

Along the Mersey, on whose banks, fringed with rich foliage, is the familiar shore or sand of New Brighton, quite gay with a crowd of holiday-makers; then we pass the old Formby light-ship; now we are running at full speed along the Welsh coast (quite near our neighbour ship still), the mountains looking their best this glorious, sunny, breezy afternoon. And what a range for grand solid mass and sweeping outline is the Snowdon group. There is Carnedd Lewellyn and Carnedd Dafydd, up whose ancient summits our children were climbing the other day, and there the long and yellow sands of Penmaenmawr and Llanfairfechan and Aber, and the sweetly quiet old Beaumaris, with new Llandudno, queen of the Welsh sea resorts. There, too, is Puffin Island, whilst nearer stand out the sullen rocks of Anglesey. It is a day of uncommon beauty. The sky towards the west is pure clear blue, with a vast over-arching curtain of light clouds above. The mountain sides and the green valleys shine in the sunlight. Over all blows the delicious south-west wind.

Day at last dies away, and with the dusk come out the everlasting stars and a pale moon. As darkness overspreads us the ship's track is visible by the white foam and flashes of phosphorescence seen in our wake, which are very beautiful to look upon. And then from the heavenly constellations our eyes descend, and those careful watch-lights, like friendly stars, flash frequently in sight. How much of forethought there is on every jutting headland and on many dangerous reefs round these sea-dashed islands! Every night a thousand lights flash around our coast to warn from danger, and to guide the path of the departing or returning mariner. How little we know or think, who live our lives in great cities, what a world of experience has been crystallised into life-saving appliances like the South Stack and Eddystone lighthouses! It was with such thoughts as these that I went down into my comfortable cabin to rest and refreshing sleep. The south-west wind brought on its wings rain clouds that cooled the night air, and in the morning (Sunday), when I awoke about seven, we were running through unusually heavy rain.

At eight the clouds had broken, the sky dappled blue and white, a fresh breeze was blowing, and we sailed into the magnificent harbour of Queenstown, where the mightiest navy in the world might safely ride at anchor. The long line of sweeping hills, many crowned with dense wood, and all dotted with white-looking houses, make a beautiful picture—Queenstown crowning the picture like Constantinople in the centre of the Golden Horn.

The air is laden with sweet odours from the land. The bay is peopled with many ships and small craft at anchor or gliding across its almost unruffled surface. Seagulls in thousands float and fly and flutter around. Small boats laden with fresh vegetables and fruits come near. The sun shines, and every man, woman, and child on board the ship is delighted and happy. The passengers' letters arrive—they are from New York—what a rush of those who are going home! Many anxieties are hushed and some brought to light by this arrival. I see in some eyes tears of gratitude, and in others sadness at news of sudden care and trouble.

II. ACROSS THE ATLANTIC.

ABOUT three o'clock in the afternoon, our tender came alongside, bringing the English mail and more passengers, as well as those who had gone ashore for the morning. What a mass of correspondence there is in those bags—quite a deckfull of huge bags of letters ! These are the threads, which carried by the steam shuttle of an ocean steamer, are perpetually weaving between the two English-speaking countries, bonds that can never be broken. The last packages at length are brought on board, the great anchor is lifted up, and we move out of the harbour towards the Atlantic, our tender going in company a short way, and then we are alone. The last light, Fastnet, fades in the dim distance as the moon rises and the stars appear in a clear, cold, grey sky : the wind is freshening, and the white rolling waves are gathering force, as if for a trial of strength with our floating home. As we had passed away from the shelving coast of Old Ireland, green and fresh with the spray of the unresting Atlantic wave, shoals of porpoises disported themselves alongside, and actually crossed the path of the ship. Later in the evening we were all delighted by the sight of a true lunar rainbow which spanned the heavens. With night came rough winds and the discomfort of the sea. The next morning there were many sickly faces and not a large gathering at breakfast ; for the sea was sullen and the sky without sun. As the day advanced, it might be truly said of the merriest man of the previous night, "he had a subdued air." Such is the effect of a troubled sea.

Monday we ran 258 miles ; Sunday 252. But there was little incident to record. All nature was somewhat leaden in colour. Tuesday morning was brighter and brought evidence of improvement on all sides. Sunshine, less rush and whirl of water alongside, more disposition to talk and be cheerful : glass rising. But no festive board for more than a select and seasoned few ; the rest of our company may be found in quiet nooks and corners huddled under wraps on chairs and such like, hugging their private griefs, each in his or her own peculiar way. And so the second day out of Queenstown passed.

Wednesday brought us lighter air, smooth seas, brilliant sky, exuberant spirits. What a wonderful change! The grand ship herself seemed nerved with a new force and pushed forward with added majesty and grace. Little festivities go forward on board. Games unseen before are played on deck. Cards and a variety of games appear. Singing, tale-telling, good humour, merry laughter of girls, and all that speaks of joyous feeling pervades the numerous company. Places yesterday vacant at table are now occupied at breakfast, lunch, and dinner, and a murmur of congratulations makes musical the saloon. And so the day goes on; the sunshine fades, the stars and moon sail into the quiet heavens, and in the stillness of the sea and air, the only sound is the throbbing of that great iron heart, the pulsations of which push us on our watery way.

Thursday morning dawns grey and misty; a thin film hangs over the vast expanse of ocean, and our fog-horn is sounded each minute. Now those who bid high for the high figures last night at the auction of distances run by the ship during the twenty-fours, ending at twelve noon to-day, are somewhat disheartened, and those who held by the lower figures are equally elated. I must explain. On certain evenings a number of figures, say 305 to 335 (that is thirty numbers), are offered by auction—that figure, say 331 or 317, which represents the actual run of the ship, taking the result of the auction. The thing is very amusing to witness; but as the man said who had never seen loo played before, "It's very like gambling." Our run was announced to have been 336 miles.

Friday morning opened brilliantly; a soft south-west wind brought a delicious coolness, needed to mitigate the sun's heat. A cloudless sky overarched the vast expanse of deep blue sea. On either bow of the vessel, at some distance, three ships in full sail glided along, whilst far away the masts of a large receding vessel barred the horizon. My sea-going friends told me that this was an unusual sight in mid-ocean, and I had been surprised that we had seen so few vessels since leaving Queenstown.

We are a varied company. Almost all the nationalities of Europe are represented; many ladies, some beautiful and accomplished and young, who favour us with music and sing; others, like too many in the world, prosaic and prudish to an extent not pleasant. Of men there are only two or three who may be called disagreeable, whilst there are some who possess and practise all the Christian virtues; and on board ship there is great scope for such experience. My friend of sea experiences again tells me that he has never, during his many voyages, been in so delightful a ship's company, so that I feel I am enjoying a sail of more than ordinary attractiveness. At all events I can say truly that the last four days have been among the happiest days of my life. With congenial human society, under sunny skies upon the untroubled ocean,—

> "What more felicity can fall to creature,
> Than to enjoy delight with liberty?"

And the deep undercurrent of feeling, the diapason to all this melodious life, which runs homeward to those we hold most dear, is never absent, as well as the lighter and hopeful thoughts of what pleasant meetings of welcome are in store for us in the West.

In crossing the Atlantic in this grand ship, so abundantly provided with all the conveniences and comforts—nay, even luxuries of life, one cannot help looking back to the early days of our great seamen, the days of Frobisher, Drake, and Raleigh, and wondering at their doings in their insignificant boats. Truly they were men of heroic hearts, who went forth hungering for adventure and discovery, wrestling with difficulties and dangers such as are not easily realized by the modern mind. Out of the strong will and endeavour of those earlier days have grown the marvels of our own times. The epic of steel and steam has, however, yet to be written.

We are in the Gulf Stream, and the air is deliciously balmy; like moths, we are all brought on deck by the glitter of the sunlight, and there is a general feeling throughout the company that they would like it to be always afternoon. We are quite a company of Lotos eaters, and feel like work no more. With evening came rain, driving us to the saloon and smoke-room for our amusements, and succeeding the rain came winds to help us on our way as well as to send many to bed. Saturday brought more rain and a heavy atmosphere, which caused us all to look "sicklied o'er with the pale cast of thought," and a general dulness supervened. Under these circumstances most people go down to write letters home, which may account for a variety of things.

The evening of Saturday, 18th September, when we had been a week at sea, was beautiful. The sun went down behind a bank of cloud in yellow radiance, leaving a cold, clear sky, into which presently sailed the full-orbed moon, golden in colour, and large, the harvest moon of England, followed shortly by Jupiter, brilliant amongst the starry host. We sat on deck watching the wonders of the night until the moon had reached high in the heavens, and only the midnight hour and the now chilly air sent us to bed. Sunday opened fittingly after a superb night; the sky a silver grey, such as is never seen in England; the sea deep blue, the horizon sharply defined; a delicious breeze sweeping over all; all our little colony full of cheerfulness and happy faces at breakfast, and afterwards walking on the spacious deck, which is one of the chief advantages a Cunard boat has over those of the other lines. At 10.30 we went down to the saloon, where a Church of England service was held—the captain reading prayers, an American clergyman preaching, a few ladies and gentlemen acting as choir, with a piano accompaniment. It is a beautiful and touching sight to witness out here in the North Atlantic Ocean a household, for we may call ourselves one, gathering together and lifting up their hearts and voices to the Infinite Father, and pouring forth, each in its own way, some feeling of gratitude for the many enjoyments of sight and sound which had followed us daily. The captain, like the father of the family, was our mouthpiece, and prayed from the heart; manliness and simplicity are in him richly combined. The soul-penetrating hymn, "Nearer, my God, to Thee," lifted all of us into a region at one with the sea, and sunlight, and the illimitable vault of heaven. As the day advanced, so grew the wonderful beauty of the sea and sky. The immense vault of blue seemed lifted immeasurably higher, and the circling sea took colour more intense. As evening came and the sun disappeared beyond the sea, rich orange hues overspread the western sky, and, as on the previous night, the golden moon sailed grandly into sight, followed by many stars.

These descriptions, no doubt, are very much alike day by day, but, remember, our only companions are the sea and sky, and some of us are seeing these majestic wonders almost for the first time. Let not those who live in cities imagine they know the boundless wealth of beauty and grandeur which the heavens disclose unless they have been across the great deep. I never before so fully realised as during this voyage the meaning of Wordsworth, when he says :—

> "And I have felt
> A presence that disturbs me with the joy
> Of elevated thoughts; a sense sublime
> Of something far more deeply interfused,
> Whose dwelling is the light of setting suns,
> And the round ocean, and the living air,
> And the blue sky, and in the mind of man :
> A motion and a spirit that impels
> All thinking things, all objects of all thought,
> And rolls through all things."

Grand as have been the days and nights through which we have passed, a fresh and great delight was experienced this morning, when, at six o'clock, I went on deck and saw the sun rise out of the sea, filling the sky with splendour beyond speech or pen. Crimson and gold and blue in the east, pale delicate colours with a fading moon in the west. All that the poets have sung of the Golden Gates of day was revealed in this transcendent transfiguring sunrise. The happy hours flew past; ships with their white wings spread moved along the horizon; butterflies came fluttering about the ship, a bird alighted on the mast, but seeing a white-sailed vessel at no great distance flew there. There is a busy movement of passengers suddenly. What is happening? The man on the look-out cries out, and the word "Pilot" is in every mouth. Presently we see a small four-oared boat like a speck ahead; it has put off from a lugger standing off a mile or so. Now we approach the boat, the boatmen ply their oars vigorously, the great engines are stopped, a rope is thrown and a rope-ladder let down the ship's side. The pilot seizes the thrown rope and swings himself dextrously and with skill on to the ladder and in a trice is on board. The boat is cast off, the huge engines turn, we are again on our way, but a new feeling pervades the vessel. We have, although four hundred miles and more away from land, grasped hands with the American Continent. As evening comes on we run into fog and rain. But indoors we are having "high jinks," for the young people have got up an entertainment, and music, singing, and recitations, in which our good captain joins, are carried on until a late hour.

III. ARRIVAL AT NEW YORK.

NOTHING could be more delightful than the fresh morning, the last of our voyage, on which we approached Sandy Hook. For several hours everybody was on the look-out upon deck with happy faces; towards evening, as we looked upon the wood-crowned heights of New Jersey, a deep crimson overspread the sky, and the sun went down in unwonted splendour. Slowly we steamed by the great forts, which guard the entrance at the "narrows," to the inner bay of New York, now fringed with many lights. The bay of New York is large and beautiful, capable of harbouring the fleets of the world. Shortly after six o'clock we dropped anchor, not being allowed to pass the quarantine ground after sundown, as the Americans say. It was a lovely scene—the glow of the setting sun had not faded before the moon rose over Brooklyn, the numerous ships hung out their lights, and the encircling shore sparkled like an illumination.

It is difficult to describe our feelings at a time of excitement such as is experienced upon reaching port after a voyage—people are all happy, and are not afraid to show it. My American friends, especially the ladies, were eager to know of course how I liked their country—at first sight—before I had set foot upon it, and I could answer readily and with truth, that the first near look at the continent made me realise vividly that I was entering a New World.

It was late that night before the company could settle down to rest, and it certainly seemed hard that after crossing the Atlantic and touching the shore as it were, we must be kept from landing until to-morrow. Such, however, is Custom House fate. It was a moving sight next morning as we neared the dock side, to see the crowd of friends looking out for those who had been across the sea, and the respective recognitions as face caught sight of face from ship to shore. Generally we see more rejoicing however than sadness, for here parents meet children, brothers their sisters, husbands their wives; "there is dear grandmother," says one little fellow; "here is father," says another.

At last we say farewell to the good ship *Scythia*, to her excellent captain, and to the friends who have been our companions during the voyage; and set foot upon the continent of America.

We are in New York, the greatest port of the United States, and one of the capitals of the world—comparatively a place of yesterday, and yet how vast a growth! No place I have seen reminds me of Paris so much as New York. It is a mixture of English, Dutch, and French seaports, the French element predominating. Land having become valuable, the buildings stretch towards heaven. We went to the top of one of these high towers—the Equitable Life Offices in Broadway—whence there is a bird's-eye view of New York, New Jersey, Brooklyn, the Hudson and East rivers, the wooded country inland, and the bay, with Staten Island and the Atlantic beyond. It is a wonderfully beautiful sight.

I am not going to undertake a description of New York, but I must mention a few points which to me were striking. For instance, nothing in my experience can be worse than the paving of the streets of this great city. It is simply execrable, and renders quick movement in a carriage impossible. But to some extent there is compensation in the net work of trams which are everywhere. There is also the elevated railway, which runs above the sidewalks; and there are the stages, as they call the shabby London omnibuses. The names over shop doors are curious and new; few old English names, many German, some Dutch, and numerous Jewish.

The Post-office is an admirable institution, and I could not help feeling strongly how slow we are at home to take new ways, and how readily an American adopts the best method. For instance, in the sorting of letters and in the matter of private boxes for firms at the Post-office. Here each firm or individual has a small box, the inside of which he can see. In case there are letters for him he unlocks the box and takes them. There are many thousands of these boxes. With us in "practical" Manchester we have our boxes into which are sorted the letters of our firms, but a staff of clerks has to be kept to hand out the letters, taking up time and space unnecessarily.

Central Park is a grand lung to New York, containing 1,500 acres, laid out on the English landscape style, and is a pleasure ground for rich and poor, who resort to it in thousands. Dotted over the city are many squares, called parks, and on the side walks of numerous streets are planted trees.

Theatres abound. We went to the opera-house, and saw our countrywoman Ada Cavendish in a play called *The Soul of an Actress*, which made one wonder that a woman with genius should spend her strength on such poor stuff. The audience was large and such as would certainly not be seen in any theatre in England, probably not in any theatre in Europe. There were no " gods," but the whole house was occupied by respectably-dressed, well-mannered people. We were played out as one is after service at church by the orchestra, a novel and pleasing feature. I afterwards looked in for an hour at a music saloon—large, well filled, elegantly decorated, lighted with the electric light, first-class music well given, and perfectly respectable. Afterwards we had an oyster supper at a crowded place in Broadway; the same good conduct and respectable people everywhere. Such places in our own country would all have in them a leaven of loud vulgarity and snobbishness to say the least. Here at all events democracy vindicates itself. There is, I admit, at least visible, less of what we should call high culture, but, on the other hand, there is a vastly greater number of instructed and happy people. Such were my feelings on this night, and subsequent similar experiences have confirmed my early impressions. In the streets, in the horse-cars, in the railways, at the theatres, at church, in all places where people meet together, there is a more serious air than is found in similar gatherings at home.

I have just returned from a visit to Coney Island, Manhattan Beach; a new seaside watering place, about an hour distant by ferry and rail from New York. It is a series of stupendous hotels upon the seashore, beginning at one end with a select sort of Fifth Avenue style of place and graded down to most popular requirements. You may walk several miles along the beach, and a very large portion of the sea terrace is laid down in grassy turf, richly ornamented with beds of flowers. To Manchester people, Belle Vue will give some idea of what preparations are necessary for feeding a large crowd, but Belle Vue never had two hundred thousand visitors in one day as was the case here, 4th July, 1880. Forty thousand people could not get back, and had to remain out encamped as well as they could for the whole summer night. All manner of amusements are provided, and there are extraordinary facilities for feeding these summer crowds. But the grand charm of the place, beyond the fine music morning and afternoon, is the long line of shore, upon which the rollers of the Atlantic beat and break.

IV. NEW ENGLAND.

LEFT New York one afternoon at five o'clock for Providence, Rhode Island, in a steamer which I believe surpasses all of its kind. There are only two others on American waters comparable to the *Massachusetts;* one being her sister boat, the other one of the Hudson river boats to Albany. Her engines are of 2,800-horse power. There is accommodation on board for 500 people; to-night we are taking over 300. Each stateroom, as it is called, is conveniently furnished, provided with a comfortable bed or beds, and is lighted with gas. The dining-room and saloons are spacious, richly decorated and appointed, and lighted with the electric light. It is the most luxurious travelling in the world. I dined at the captain's table; the bill of fare was choice but not elaborate, there were only fourteen kinds of vegetable, and the wine the best I drank in the States. These boats are much used. I was introduced to one gentleman who had been going between Providence and New York weekly for years, and he had not once slept in New York, but after finishing his business in the afternoon dined and slept on board the boat, awaking fresh for his work in good time the next morning.

It was a lovely evening as we glided from our moorings in the

Hudson River and threaded our way amidst the multitude of craft of every kind which crowd the waters of New York, and as we made our way along the East river and under the stupendous suspension bridge in construction which is to connect Brooklyn and New York, the setting sun lighted up the former city with unwonted splendour and threw New York into shadow and clear outline against the sky. No view of New York is more picturesque than this from East river by evening light. The ridge along the centre of the city upon which Broadway runs is crowned with lofty structures—spires, towers, warehouses, churches, and massive shapes in broken line—while the lower tiers of buildings in deeper shadow decline to the water's edge and mingle with the multitude of masts which stand out boldly in the foreground. It is a subject worthy of a great artist. By-and-by we are steaming past Blackwell's Island, upon which are situated the penal and correctional institutions of New York, as well as those for lunatics and paupers. For these are all needed, alas, even in the New World. Before dusk we are feeling our way carefully through Hell Gate, a narrow and dangerous shoal, the passage to the sound, where the United States Government have expended large sums, and are still at work, in blasting the hidden rocks to clear a passage and make the way safer. As evening falls the lights to mark our way appear, and by seven o'clock or so we are in the open waters of Long Island Sound. As on many nights past, when I retired to rest the full-orbed moon had sailed high into the dark blue heavens, encircled by a multitude of stars. The gentle motion of our boat rocked me, as in a cradle, to a refreshing sleep, from which I was awakened only by the stopping of our engine, as we touched the quay side of Providence, Rhode Island.

When I opened my cabin window, a rich orange glow in the eastern sky preluded the rising sun, forming a wonderful background to the picturesque outline of the city, built along a ridge and sloping to the bay. My friend living some twelve or fifteen miles away, we went, at 6-45, to the railway station (depôt they call it), where we got a comfortable breakfast. This is a feature not known to us. Early rising is common all over the States, as far as I went. The older portion of Providence is east of the bay, and here is the old State House, containing a good library and many portraits of governors of the State; also the original charter, granted in the seventeenth century. There are many fine residences on this side, a church with a beautiful tall tower and spire of wood, and what was in older days the main street. Now, however, the leading street is on the western side, on which the city has grown and is growing. Westminster is a most picturesque street, reminding me of the High Street in Oxford. On the west side also stands the City Hall, a handsome building near the railway station, and the Butler Exchange, a modern fine example of enterprise and taste in commercial building. After our drive round the town, accompanied by my American friend, I took train to the Athens of America.

Boston, to Englishmen, is probably the most interesting American city. Partly, no doubt, because of its associations historically and for its own beauty, but mainly because of the intellectual culture of its citizens, which has placed it in the van of civilization in the United States. One of the most beautiful general views of Boston is from the north-west side, on the way to Cambridge. The town clusters together upon three hills, but seen from a distance there appear to be terraces of building rising from the water to the crown of what seems one ridge, which is broken by church spires, by chimneys, by towers, by the shaft on Bunker Hill, and nearer the centre by the great gilt dome of the State House, which stands out like a vast gold crown. From South Boston, the reverse of this view is seen, with a finer foreground of water and shipping. Unlike other cities of the States, the streets run irregularly, as in English towns, except the long lines which stretch out into the suburbs. Much of the old town in the business quarters was burnt down in 1874, and has been rebuilt in a style unsurpassed by any city in the world. We have some elegant warehouses in Manchester, and there are not a few in various cities in the provinces which are admirable, as well as in London; but I have no hesitation in saying that the magnificent white and variegated marble and granite palaces erected in Boston for business and State purposes are grander than any we have in Great Britain, and rival those of the most illustrious cities of Italy.

The marble structures of Boston are simply wonderful. I was taken on to the towers of one of these lofty buildings, the Mutual Insurance Offices I think, and saw the city like a map at our feet, the Charles river, the Common, and the Park, the distant hills, the harbour and bay, and the glistening far-off sea. My Boston friends may well be proud of their city. Boston Common is a grand open of about fifty acres in this bustling centre. And I think it never looked finer than when I saw those majestic elms and oaks, which are the glory of the place, transfigured by radiant autumnal colour. In the streets, too, are glorious old trees. From the window of the hotel, as I dined or made notes on the passing stream of human life, I looked upon a grand old tree in the space before one of the public offices. It may possibly interest some of my friends to learn what an American hotel is like. When you arrive, you walk up to the counter of the office in the hall and enter your name and address. You have a room allotted to you, your baggage is taken up by a lift, you are taken up by another. Lifts are almost in universal use. You are charged so many dollars a day, say from two and a half dollars to five dollars, according to the style of room. This includes all your eating. There is very little drinking in any hotel I was in during my visit. I was never asked by a waiter, during my stay, what I would take to drink, nor shown a wine list unless I asked for one. This is common sense. Can any traveller for a month in England say this?

Breakfast is generally served from seven to nine ; railway breakfasts earlier. Lunch, one to three ; dinner, five to seven ; supper, nine to eleven o'clock. As a waiter said to me in New York, " You may begin to eat here, sir, at five o'clock in a morning, and go on until midnight !" In the hall there is usually a cigar and tobacco stall, a newspaper boy, ticket offices for theatres and railways, and a reading and writing room. In the larger hotels the dining-rooms are upstairs. In the basement you find barbers, shoeblacks, and various conveniences. You pay ten cents each morning for having your shoes "shined." There are no tips. Englishmen, however, do tip ; ancient habits are hard to overcome. There is so much to be said on the subject of hotel feeding in the States that I will leave it for fuller treatment in a subsequent letter.

The number of people who are housed in these hotels is very large, varying in the first-class houses from 200 or 300 to 800 or 1,000. In the season at Saratoga 1,500 and 1,800 can be put up at each of the largest houses. The principal hotel at Richmond, Virginia, can take in 800. I suppose the Parker House, at which I stayed at Boston, could accommodate several hundred people ; it is usually full, and is said to be a prosperous concern.

No building in Boston excites more interest in admirers of America than Faneuil Hall, "the cradle of liberty," which stands in the centre of the business quarter of the city, a plain, solid, almost square block. Here the citizens met in the early days of the struggle for independence, and here, in later and equally stirring times, the cause of the slave has been eloquently pleaded. It was for a speech in Faneuil Hall against kidnapping, that Theodore Parker was tried at Boston in 1855. And twenty years before, the walls of Faneuil Hall had echoed to a famous orator of Boston on behalf of slavery and slaveholders, the Hon. Peleg Sprague, who proclaimed a new gospel, "Slaves, obey your masters !" At that very time the State of Georgia was offering 5,000 dollars for the head of William Lloyd Garrison ! It seems incredible that so great a change can have been worked out in so short a time as twenty-five years. Thank God ! the bondsman has been made free, and the reign of cruelty is at an end. With John Bright, "I believe there was no mode short of a miracle more stupendous than any recorded in Holy Writ that could in our time have brought about the abolition of slavery in America, but the suicide which the South committed and the war which it began."

V. NEW ENGLAND.

ONE of the most delightful incidents of my too brief stay in New England was a visit to Longfellow, who lives on the way to Mount Auburn, a short distance beyond Cambridge. It was a lovely morning ; the magnificent forest trees around Harvard University and along the road were rich in many-coloured foliage, the glory of New England during the Indian summer. The poet's house stands in its own grounds, a little way from the road, and is embosomed in trees, with a pleasant lawn-like greenery before it. As he has written:—

> "Somewhat back from the village street,
> Stands the old-fashioned country seat;
> Across its antique portico
> Tall poplar trees their shadows throw."

It was the head-quarters of General Washington during the siege of Boston. A view of distant hills is seen from the grounds, looking south. At the garden gate we were met by Mr. Longfellow, who led us back to the house and into his library. I noticed a fine portrait of Emerson when young, as well as one of the Poet himself of similar date; also a statuette of Goethe. The room was just what one might have pictured—not large, but cosy and well filled with books, with a comfortable, plain writing table, and the arm-chair made from the wood of the village blacksmith's chestnut tree, presented to Longfellow on his seventy-second birthday, 27th February, 1879, by the children of Cambridge. There, too, was the old clock on the stairs, of which he has sung:—

> "Half-way up the stairs it stands,
> And points and beckons with its hands,
> From its case of massive oak,
> And from its station in the hall,
> The ancient timepiece says to all,
> For ever—never! Never—for ever!"

One of our party, an American, read aloud the poem "Jugurtha," from the volume *Ultima Thule*, then just published in Boston, copies of which were on the table.

I told the poet how much I felt myself indebted to him for many, many happy hours; how his writings had often comforted me in sorrow and amidst the worry and distraction of daily work; and that in my home, as I believed in tens of thousands of homes in the Old Country, was realized his wish when he wrote—

> "Therefore I hope, as no unwelcome guest
> At your warm fireside, when the lamps are lighted,
> To have my place reserved among the rest,
> Nor stand as one unsought and uninvited."

I had long looked forward to a visit to Concord and to Cambridge, and I felt when the Poet took my hand to bid me farewell, that my voyage across the Atlantic had not been in vain—

> "For they shall be accounted Poet-Kings
> Who simply tell us most heart-easing things!"

I left Boston with deep regret. There were so many friends unseen, so much of interest, of instruction, and of pleasure, had to be postponed until my next visit. Here, as I found afterwards everywhere, my American friends were all kindness and hospitality—with a love for the Old Country like our own.

I spent my first Sunday in the States at a charming quiet seaside place called Warren-neck, to which I was driven about a dozen miles from a considerable group of manufacturing villages, in the Pawtucket Valley. At Harrisville, where my friend lives, I had opportunity for observing how much more comfortably placed are those engaged in the cotton manufacture than those so occupied at home, especially in our large towns. There each man has a detached dwelling, with a small plot of ground. Many of the houses are the property of the occupiers. The hours of labour are longer than with us, but the workers are by no means less intelligent, and are strong and healthy, for they live in a purer air and in a more tranquil moral atmosphere. The schoolhouse has not been planted for generations in New England in vain.

Warren-neck is a strip of rocky coast stretching from the mainland into an arm of Long Island Sound, and in the season is a place of daily resort for many thousands from Providence, and other towns, who have a shore dinner of clam chowder, for the cooking of which great preparations are made. It is a kind of mixture like mussels and cockles stewed with vegetables, and is capital eating. The use of the telephone is much more general on the other side than with us. At dinner we drank the health of a young lady friend who lived some twenty miles away, and whilst our hostess remained at the instrument a minute or two an answer came thanking us for our remembrance of her. So, on my arrival in Providence, a day or two before, I had been welcomed by my friend's wife, who was at breakfast, fourteen miles away.

On Monday the steamer from Providence to Newport touched at Warren-neck, taking us on board. An hour's sail landed us at the most celebrated seaside resort in the States. Newport is without doubt a charming place. The walk along the rocks overlooking the sea, with fine villa residences near, and a grand greensward, such as we have in England, reaching a few miles, makes a most loveable spot, where one could readily forget much of this world's worries and cares, but for the excessive display which disports itself. The same enterprise which has worked wonders in steamboats and railways across the continent has made the barren rocky side of Newport one of the most delightful walks in the world. But to be a Newporter properly one must have, I should say, not less than £10,000 a year. The town of Newport is old. There is a newspaper here, which was established by Benjamin Franklin. The main street, and much of the rocky character of the place, reminded me of Ilfracombe, North Devon.

In the evening we returned to Warren-neck, and then drove across country to my friend's house at Harrisville, about twelve miles inland. On various parts of the drive we passed coloured squatters' little places, as well as large farms, well cultivated. Passed numerous orchards, too, where the trees were literally crushed down beneath the weight of ripened fruit. It is a great apple year. A lady friend told me that apples had been selling at the orchards at three cents a bushel. Two generations ago the Red Indian was here, but the white man has pushed him back westward, and is fast civilising him with spirits and other things off the face of the earth.

I took the cars (as they call a train) one morning at Providence, and set off on my own account. Hitherto I had been taken in hand by my excellent friend Governor Howard, of Providence, R.I., whom I was to rejoin in a day or two. A couple of hours brought me to Worcester, a genuine Puritan old city, peopled by some of the old Plymouth Rock stock. Never have I seen more magnificent trees than those on each side of the principal street. They reminded me of the trees at Oxford on the Broad Walk. The place was all alive, like market-day in one of our Midland Counties market towns, and had a solid, substantial, respectable air. But the foliage which pervades the city gives it a character of its own, and is more suggestive of Germany and France than our own country. The people are, however, more English-looking than any I have seen. The streets are wide, with fine shops and warehouses. Here, as elsewhere, is a soldiers' monument, and recalls the memory of those whose deeds their fellow-citizens would not willingly let die.

After the manner of Americans who "do" England in about three days, I was obliged to push on, reaching the fine railway depôt just in time for one of the fast Boston to Albany and New York trains. Fruit is plentiful at the railway station, and I lay in a stock of apples, pears, grapes, and peaches for fifty cents. This is a populous district, and the cars are well filled with intelligent, well-dressed, comfortable, but apparently serious people. Six or seven long American cars, through which you can walk, make our train, the seats arranged for two run down each side the car, with a central aisle. Nearly all are filled. We run through undulating, well-wooded country, glowing with warm colour. The most brilliant crimsons and scarlets and every conceivable shade of yellow and brown and green are painted on the thick woods, and with a foreground of dark soil or verdant meadow, make a picture no man has dared to paint and none have ventured fully to describe. This is the land of colour at this autumn season. I saw a lady with the bough of a tree as large as she could carry—every leaf bright yellow, but tinted round the edges brilliant carmine. It was a mass of beauty, and drew attention even in that locality. I begged a few leaves as a memento : they are still beautiful, although, like pearly shells we gather on the shore, they suffer from absence of sunlight.

"Springfield !" calls the conductor. They call out after leaving each station what the next will be, so as to give travellers time to prepare for leaving. Another busy, thriving city, with main street, by name and in reality, running north and south. Here is the United States arsenal and gun factory, where large quantities of warlike material can be produced. Before the slaveholders' revolt, and during the last months of the Buchanan administration, immense loads of arms and ammunition were moved away from Springfield to Southern cities, to the astonishment and consternation of its peaceful, Union-loving citizens. There are also large watch manufactories here. Trees give picturesqueness to the streets as well as shade from the hot sun of summer. Within the distance of an hour's drive I had a view from high land overlooking the Connecticut valley, and a more magnificent prospect I had not seen in the country. Far away as the eye could trace flowed the river in each direction, north and south, and when the faint shimmer of the water was no more seen, the distant forest-clad mountains seemed to rest against the soft grey sky of evening.

It was to a visit to Springfield that I had for many years looked forward, for here had lived my friend Samuel Bowles, well known all over the States, and loved wherever known. In the great battle of life he had fought hard and nobly in support of those principles of justice and freedom, without which the United States would have become like a rope of sand. The strain laid upon that refined and highly-strung organization was too severe, and he passed away, alas! too soon. I had felt that America could not be quite the same to me without my friend. And it was with a heart tremulous with emotion that I entered the place which knew him no more. There I found those my friend had left behind, and around whom, for his sake, my affections had long grown; with whom, after many greetings and much unconcealed sadness, I spent some happy hours, the memory of which will never pass away.

The time here was, alas! too short, and as night approached I was once more on the convenient iron way, which has so quickly brought all the world nearer together, and after four hours reached delightful New Haven, called for the best of reasons, the Elm City. Even Worcester, which I left this morning, so rich in trees, cannot vie with the magnificent avenues of ancient elms which encircle the college buildings of Yale, and lift their spreading arms across the city green. Then, outside this charming city, which looks upon the sea, are far stretching woods inland, through which we drive, and beyond these rise grand bluffs, called East and West Rocks, which made my heart leap as I saw them first from the railway carriage, reminding me of the banks of our own Wye in Monmouthshire. Ah! I shall always treasure the memory of my drive under the elms of New Haven and through her brilliant woods, and under the shadow of her rough bold rocks. It was a happy termination to my brief visit to New England, the home of merry, loving, tender, affectionate, and cultivated men and women, whom I am proud to call my friends.

VI. PHILADELPHIA.

AMONG the many novel and interesting sights in New York few took my fancy more than the grand ferries, which ply continually between Brooklyn and New York, and between New York and Jersey City. Over the Hudson river in this last-named ferry I started one fine morning on the way to Washington. The ferry is an immense floating pier, upon which passengers, carriages and horses, carts, drays, and in some cases complete trains of railway carriages, are taken bodily across the broad rivers. New York, Brooklyn, Jersey City, and Newark, being all within the distance of a few miles, there is always sufficient movement of population and its requirements on the rivers which girdle New York, to find constant work for these unique, leviathan craft.

The Pennsylvania railroad service is one of the finest in the United States, and after leaving Jersey City we were carried along at a pace of forty miles an hour for considerable time, over country almost as flat as Lincolnshire. As we approach Philadelphia, the aspect of the country is more varied, and becomes picturesque. The Quaker City is built on the Schuylkill and Delaware rivers, a few miles above their confluence, and about one hundred miles from the sea. The shipping on these rivers, anchored at the city wharves, especially on the Delaware, tell their own story of the commercial importance of Philadelphia. It is the chief outlet for the products of the state of Pennsylvania, rich in coal and iron. Marble too is here in abundance, one of the noted features of the city being the profusion of white marble used in building. Every house in the principal streets has a flight of marble steps. The beautiful mansion of Mr. Childs, of the *Philadelphia Ledger* (like that of A. T. Stewart in New York), is built of pure white marble. The Girard College, perhaps the finest building in the country, is a magnificent Greek Temple in white marble.

Philadelphia had a great attraction for me, but whether it was the genial hospitality of the people or the air of comfort, indeed refinement, pervading the place that most charmed, I am not able to determine. The streets are somewhat narrower than in New York, but they are handsome, well-paved, and peopled with a well-dressed, unhasting crowd. It is also pleasant to find the streets named otherwise than numerically in an American city—

> "Arch and market, chestnut, vine,
> Walnut, Girard, spruce, and pine."

Some such couplet was given me to indicate the leading streets. Along the main thoroughfares run horse tram-cars, and excellent carriages are on hire at call. The hotels here are most desirable resting-places.

The centre of interest in Philadelphia was Independence Hall, a plain, brick building, with a picturesque tower surmounted by a belfry, in which formerly was hung the great city bell, having on it this inscription, "Liberty throughout the land unto all the inhabitants thereof." The Declaration of Independence was issued here on the 4th July, 1776, and here, too, during the early years of its institution, the United States Congress assembled. Various relics of those past days are shown. The quiet quadrangle upon which this building looks is made beautiful by spreading trees and shady walks.

Besides the various squares, which act as breathing spaces, Philadelphia possesses the most magnificent public park probably in the world. Stretching along both banks of the Schuylkill river—in itself a source of delight to the eye,—the Fairmount Park embraces in its area of four thousand acres almost every variety of natural beauty, and contributes pleasure to thousands of people daily all the year round. Another sylvan opening is the park-like enclosure which surrounds that grand institution, Girard College, the extent and magnificence of which may perhaps be suggested by the statement that the structure alone cost more than the sum left by Girard for the purpose, viz., two millions of dollars. The foundation stone was laid in July, 1833, and the main building was completed and transferred to the directors 13th November, 1847. The institution is sustained principally from the rental of real estate left by the founder, Stephen Girard. Two hundred orphans were admitted the first year, the second year another hundred were taken in, and at the present time about six hundred "poor white male orphans" find a home, and are "maintained and educated" there. "No uniform or distinctive dress is permitted to be worn." The boys may at stated times visit and be visited by their friends. When the time arrives many are indentured by the College to learn some trade or occupation. Professors, male and female teachers, doctors, a dentist, and a steward have charge of their respective departments, as well as a matron, prefects, and governesses for the household, the whole government of the College being vested in the president, who is the chief executive officer of the institution, and is responsible for its proper administration. Strangers, with a permit, are admitted any day between nine a.m. and sunset. The special feature in Girard's will is contained in the following clause: "I enjoin and require that no ecclesiastic, missionary, or minister of any sect whatsoever, shall ever hold or exercise any station or duty whatever in the said College; nor shall any such person ever be admitted for any purpose, or as a visitor, within the premises appropriated to the purposes of the said College. In making this restriction, I do not mean to cast any reflection upon any sect or person whatsoever; but as there is such a multitude of sects, and such a diversity of opinion amongst them, I desire to keep the tender minds of the orphans, who are to derive advantage from this bequest, free from the excitement which clashing doctrines and sectarian controversy are so apt to produce; my desire is, that all the instructors and teachers in the College shall take pains to instil into the minds of the scholars the purest principles of morality, so that on their entrance into active life they may, from inclination and habit, evince benevolence towards their fellow-creatures, and a love of truth, sobriety, and industry, adopting at the same time such religious tenets as their matured reason may enable them to prefer."

Stephen Girard was a native of Bordeaux, where he was born in 1750. He was a seafaring man, and afterwards a merchant and banker, and was entirely what is called "self-made." He died in 1831 at Philadelphia, of which place he had been a citizen about fifty years. He left at his death property valued at about seven and a half millions of dollars, the bulk of which he devised for public and benevolent purposes. I have dwelt upon Stephen Girard and the college he founded at considerable length, because of the impression made upon me by the man and his work, which is so prominently before the world in his adopted city. He was evidently a man of uncommon energy—that he had read history with care is clear from the peculiar conditions of his great bequest—and he had strong convictions and lofty purposes, along with a force of will capable of carrying them into effect, notwithstanding the prejudices by which he was surrounded. How many poor children in Manchester would the Hulme bequest have educated, had it been administered under such conditions as those of Girard's?

In July 1793, and in 1797 and '98 yellow fever visited Philadelphia and swept thousands into the grave. On the first visitation, in three months more than four thousand people perished out of a population of under 25,000. In this time of terror and confusion Girard volunteered his services to superintend the fever hospital, and by his self-devotion worked wonders in staying the pestilence and in devising preventive measures. The Apostle James tells us that "pure religion and undefiled before God and the Father is this—to visit the fatherless and widows in their affliction, and to keep himself unspotted from the world."

VII. WASHINGTON AND RICHMOND.

LEAVING Philadelphia as evening approached, I saw little in the country we were carried through to excite attention, except at Havre de Grace, where the wide, tumultuous, rock-bound Susquehanna river falls into Chesapeake Bay, along which, with frequent glimpses seaward, we travel towards Baltimore.

Baltimore is a large busy city, with considerable manufactures, and a magnificent harbour, peopled with a crowd of shipping. Coal in vast quantities is sent down to this port for shipment. The absence of trees in the streets is striking, and the general appearance of this city is plainer than those I have recently visited. We went to the theatre—Ford's Grand Opera House—and saw a musical absurdity, which pleased the audience. There was some special local gathering, and the large hotel at which we stayed was full, which gave me an opportunity of judging from large numbers indoors, as well as from my observations in the theatre and in the streets, and the impression I received was that the people were what I may describe as a "louder" toned type than any I had before seen in the States. There was also a somewhat excited state of public feeling, consequent on preparations for the celebration of the 150th year of the foundation of the city. The "sesquicentennial" was to occupy about ten days, when holiday demonstrations of every conceivable kind would be made. It was here that I made acquaintance with mosquito curtains, and had shutters to my bedroom windows to keep out the sunlight, I suppose, and I began to have a feeling that I was getting South. I could not forget that here, in the first days of the rebellion, a Massachusetts regiment, in passing through, was fired upon and mobbed.

There was not a cloud in the sky as we passed out of the suburbs of Baltimore into the open country. The train was well filled, and I soon found myself engaged in conversation with a well-known ex-Confederate General. He frankly accepted the results of the Civil War to have been the destruction of slavery and the consolidation of the Union, and that secession had brought nothing but misfortune and ruin to all engaged. He spoke as one who believed that the people in the South were so convinced, and I asked him whether there were any Southern cities in which a statue to Abraham Lincoln had been erected, as I had scarcely been in any city since my arrival in which there was not one. "Yes," he said, "in New Orleans, I believe." "I hope," said I, "the time will come when many others will follow the example of the Crescent City." I was thus engaged when my friend drew me to the window of the carriage and I saw, afar off, but beautifully distinct in the morning light, the white marble dome of the Capitol at Washington. It was a moment of supreme pleasure, such as the Catholic pilgrim may feel as he first comes in sight of St. Peter's at Rome, or the Alpine climber who sees Mont Blanc from Geneva.

The entrance into Washington by the Baltimore and Ohio railway is disappointing. Small, mean houses and other buildings surround you, and on one side almost invade the precincts of the Capitol, which rises grandly above all other objects. I have never seen magnificence and meanness so inappropriately near. No doubt, as time goes on, all this will be changed, and the land now owned by individuals will be purchased by the State, or private enterprise will exert itself, so that fitting adjuncts may entirely surround this grandest legislative palace. The scale on which the city has been laid out will require fifty years for its harmonious development, and it takes a day or so for your eye to become reconciled to the anomalies. But standing on the marble terrace in front of the Capitol, which stands on the highest ground in the city, you look on all sides upon broad avenues and "magnificent distances." Right in front, about a mile distant, is the Treasury, like a Greek temple. Beyond it are the other public offices, a vast pile of marble; and beyond these again crowds of forest trees, painted with autumn tints, half hide the White House, the official residence of the President of the United States. On the bank of the Potomac is the immense Washington monument, that promises, like Cologne Cathedral, to take ages to complete.

There are about six hundred women clerks employed in the Treasury, chiefly in the bank-note (greenback) department. In the United States no bank or banker is allowed to issue notes without depositing Government bonds as security for the amount of issue, plus ten per cent. margin; and all these bonds are kept at the Treasury. Here new notes are issued and a large stock of gold is kept. The revenue flows in here, and amounted when we were in Washington to a million dollars daily, or at the rate of seventy-six million pounds sterling a year.

It was a very agreeable experience upon walking into the Rigg's House at Washington to meet my old friends of the railway world, from Manchester. These gentlemen had been all over the Continent learning what they could from our American cousins for the benefit of English railway interests generally, and no doubt the Manchester, Sheffield, and Lincolnshire particularly.

I am not going to try even to describe the city of Washington, it has been often done, and better done than is possible by my vagrant pen. We went to the theatre, of course, took the usual drives, called upon

the British Ambassador to pay our respects, and were glad to find
that the representative of Great Britain at Washington was housed in
a style befitting old England. It may be proper here to state that in
my frequent conversations with Americans upon the question of
Ireland I never found one man or woman who had the slightest
sympathy with Parnell and the anti-rent agitation in Ireland. The
American people have too much common sense to be taken in by
bravado and tall-talk. They, too, have their own Irish question,
which is not a trifling difficulty in the great cities. In fact, it is quite
a large enough element to make the successful and permanent working
of democratic institutions still a problem of somewhat doubtful
solution.

One of the most enjoyable excursions taken from Washington is a
visit to Mount Vernon, where Washington lived and died. The road
along the Potomac is more than interesting—it would be beautiful
without a single historical association. There, close behind you, as
the steamer glides from her moorings, is the famous long bridge which
connects Virginia and Columbia, and across which the panic-stricken
hosts fled in confusion after the stampede at Bull's Run. Beyond, the
still more famous wood-crowned Arlington Heights, the residence of
the Confederate General Lee, whose genius gave a living impulse to
the heterogeneous crowd, and lifted it to the rank of a great army.
We are a mixed company on board the steamer, black and white and
half-breed, all going to the tomb of Washington. Mount Vernon is
situated on a lovely reach of the Potomac, about a dozen miles from
the city of Washington. In the grounds are several small towers, or
they may be called forts, built as outposts to be used in case of attack
from Indians in the old days. The farm buildings are extensive, and
there is a quaint piece of well-trimmed Dutch garden. Although the
mansion is not a large one, according to present fashions, it is roomy
and comfortable, and from the tower is seen a magnificent view of the
park which clusters round, of the wide and winding Potomac, Fort
Washington on the opposite bank, and of the white dome of the
distant Capitol glistening in the sunlight. In almost every room is
furniture which was there when Washington was alive. Portraits,
pictures, furniture, the bedroom in which he passed away, and in which

is framed a copy of a newspaper of the time, containing an announcement of the great man's death side by side with an advertisement of a runaway slave girl;—everything in the house is preserved with the utmost care. The property was bought some years ago with funds raised by a ladies' committee, and the various rooms and their contents, as I understood, named after the various States subscribing.

A most outrageous offence against good taste has, however, been perpetrated by those who have dared to remove the remains of Washington from the place in which he was laid, and which was most likely the spot of ground of his own choice, overlooking his favourite Potomac river. The old tomb is still there, left open and unprotected from the desecrating touch and soil of vulgar feet. And the dust of Washington, whose very name is a fragrance in all lands, has been placed with others of his kindred in a rude common brick hut, beside the carriage drive, near to the entrance of the grounds. The Americans have little sentiment and no imagination, or their reverence for the past would have prevented this desecration of the last resting-place of their most illustrious dead. An American friend, who visited Mount Vernon for the first time along with our party, and who shared my indignation, vowed that he would move his own State to obtain permission and to provide funds necessary for rescuing the ancient tomb from ruin.

We returned in the afternoon to Washington, which grows upon us every day. Time is requisite to take in these far-stretching, spacious avenues, and the colossal buildings of the State. In the evening we took the cars southward, and as the night wore on the coloured people, who were numerous in the carriage we sat in, began singing, in a plaintive, somewhat monotonous tone, but sweet and soothing. Only one line stuck to my memory, but that was many times repeated, and was very penetrating. "Shall we meet across the river?" was this melancholy refrain, and this indicates, so to speak, the moral tone of the music. With night we entered the city, and, what is not uncommon there, although unknown with us, the rails are carried along the streets at level crossings; and so, gliding slowly through gas-lighted streets, we found ourselves in the city of Richmond, Virginia. The Exchange and Ballard House, Richmond, is a typical hotel, accommodating about eight hundred guests; there were several hundreds on our arrival. Richmond is situated on high and undulating ground overlooking the river James, which flows on the south side. It is a much finer site than that Washington is built upon, and probably there is no more beautiful situation for a city in the States. The State House, as usual, is a prominent object, a plain, solid, large building surrounded by a park, in which many squirrels disport themselves around the fountains quite tame, so as to feed from the hand. From the tower of the State House one has a bird's-eye view of the city, with a widespread expanse of country, hilly and wooded; beyond, to the left, five miles or so away, is the point at which M'Clellan got hold of and stuck to Lee for six days, each army fighting and holding on to the other until exhausted, after making a fight of many miles along a line stretching east. Just below us as we stand on the roof is the church in which Jeff. Davis one Sunday morning received Lee's message from Petersburg to retire from Richmond. Not far to the left is the Libby prison, where the Confederates packed their unhappy prisoners, and where the horrors of neglect and cruelty were rampant, starvation and death being here constant companions. Near the State House is the monument to General "Stonewall" Jackson, erected by subscriptions of *English* gentlemen! Here, too, Jeff. Davis was tried for high treason, and when, at the close of the trial, the Judge announced that Davis was to enter into recognisances to appear when called upon for judgment in the sum of one hundred thousand dollars, a man in the strangers' gallery stood up and called out, "Put me down for ten thousand dollars!" It was Horace Greely. His magnanimity completely overpowered the ex-President. We also visited the inner lines of defence and various points of view of the city. Commercially there must be stagnation here. One fact impressed me strongly—except in the main lines of thoroughfares where the tramcars run, I did not see one street that was not grass grown.

The population here is about equally divided in numbers between white and coloured. On the Sunday morning I went, accompanied by one of my Manchester friends, to the Sunday-school and church of the First African Church, Richmond. There were, I suppose, about one hundred and fifty children in the school and some adults; and at the

Church, I should say, about four or five hundred were present. A young coloured man conducted the service. The people were intelligent and responsive, one could see by their faces, to the earnest exhortation which the preacher made. His text was, "Ye believe in God, believe also in me;" and in simple language, clear and forcible, he urged his hearers to cast their burden upon the Lord and believe in Him: to do their duty manfully, to speak the truth, and to live with the fear of God before their eyes. Then he said, in all your trials and daily difficulties, you may without doubt cast your burden upon Him, and He will help you; with much more to the same faithful purpose. The music—there was a choir—was simple and devotional, although somewhat drawling. There was an utter absence of noise and rant, and, as I told my friend the Rev. Brooke Herford afterwards in Chicago, from beginning to end the service was as orderly and devotional as in any cathedral in England.

VIII. HARPER'S FERRY: GETTYSBURG.

EARLY one fine morning I reluctantly said "Good-bye" to my friends at Washington, to which city I had returned from Richmond. Taking my seat in a train at the Baltimore and Ohio depôt, I travelled through cultivated country and then along the bank of the Potomac river, which grew in picturesque beauty as we neared the object of my pilgrimage, Harper's Ferry.

Harper's Ferry is a small, poor town, situated at the confluence of the Shenandoah river with the Potomac. Approached on the side nearest Washington, a steep, cone-shaped hill appears to divide the stream; the town being built along the Potomac and Shenandoah valleys, and it also straggles up and over this dividing hilly ridge, which is called Bolivar Heights. The railroad crosses the Potomac here over an iron bridge of considerable size. On the north side of the river rise craggy hills, called Maryland Heights, and on the Virginia or south side of the noisy, shallow Shenandoah river tower the wood-crowned heights of Loudon. These lofty hills on each side of the rivers give a somewhat gorge-like character to the place as seen in the valley, whilst the view from the heights, looking south and east, is wide, far-reaching, and beautiful.

It was here, in 1859, that John Brown and his score of devoted followers made their daring memorable raid. For many years John Brown was the most active agent of the so-called underground railway, of which he was the originator, and he aided many slaves to gain their freedom on British soil. His seizure of the Government arsenal at Harper's Ferry was a bold effort to rouse the slaves to strike for freedom, and may be considered the first skirmish of the great struggle then impending, which ended only when universal liberty was secured. It was a curious coincidence that the officer sent to give an account of the anti-slavery hero, and who took him prisoner in the engine house, now called John Brown's Fort, should have become the leading spirit of the army of the Confederacy, General Robert E. Lee. The life of John Brown and his execution in the State of Virginia called forth much comment by many eminent Americans. None knew him more intimately, nor aided him in his work with more cheerful liberality, than Theodore Parker, who in his last illness wrote from Rome: "No American has died this century whose chance of earthly immortality is worth half so much as John Brown's. The ex-governors of Massachusetts are half forgotten before they are wholly dead; rhetoricians and sophists are remembered while they are talking; but a man who crowns a noble life with such a glorious act as John Brown's at Harper's Ferry is not forgotten in haste. The red martyr must be a precious man. The effect is not over, nor ever will be. Brown's little spark was not put out till it had kindled a fire which will burn down much more than far-sighted men look for. The Northern sky is full of lightning long treasured up; Brown was one bright clear flash into the Southern ground. The thunder rattles all over the Union now; there will be other strokes by-and-by."

"John Brown's body lies mouldering in the grave,
But his soul is marching on!"

At Harper's Ferry, perhaps more than in any other place, is visible the ravages that terrible slaveholders' war made. In each valley were extensive national rifle manufactories, now in ruins. On the hill along which were dotted many houses, churches, and other buildings, are the shells of these structures, battered by cannon balls, and pitted all round the windows with rifle bullets. Here in 1862, the Confederates under Stonewall Jackson, having taken possession of Maryland and Loudon Heights, captured General Miles and nearly 12,000 Federals, with 73 guns, and numerous small-arms and large supplies of every kind. Two hundred and fifteen houses were destroyed, and the town simply beggared. I left this desolation in the midst of beautiful scenery in a melancholy mood, taking rail back again, alongside the Potomac a few miles, as far as Frederick city, Maryland.

Frederick was a pleasant surprise; it is a charming little town; the usual grand old trees adorn the main streets of the place, and an air of cheerfulness and solid respectability pervades the people. More than once had the war rolled through these quiet streets. Whittier has related an incident, which I will venture to quote, condensed :—

> " Up from the meadows rich with corn,
> Clear in the cool September morn,
> The clustered spires of Frederick stand,
> Green walled by the hills of Maryland.
> Round about them orchards sweep.
>
> . . . . .
>
> Over the mountains, winding down,
> Came horse and foot through Frederick town.
> Forty flags with their silver stars,
> Forty flags with their crimson bars,
> Flapped in the morning wind; the sun
> Of noon looked down, and saw not one.
> Up rose old Barbara Frietchie then,
> Bowed with her fourscore years and ten :
> Bravest of all in Frederick town,
> She took up the flag the men hauled down ;
> In her attic window the staff she set,
> To show that one heart was loyal yet.
> Up the street came the rebel tread,
> Stonewall Jackson riding ahead.
> Under his slouched hat left and right
> He glanced ; the old flag met his sight.

'Halt!'—the dust-brown ranks stood fast.
'Fire!'—out blazed the rifle blast:
It shivered the window, frame and sash;
It rent the banner with seam and gash.
Quick, as it fell, from the broken staff
Dame Barbara snatched the silken scarf;
She leaned far out on the window-sill,
And shook it forth with a royal will:
'Shoot, if you must, this old grey head,
But spare your country's flag,' she said.
A shade of sadness, a blush of shame,
Over the face of the leader came;
The nobler nature within him stirred
To life at that woman's deed and word:
'Who touches a hair of yon grey head
Dies like a dog! March on!' he said.
All day long through Frederick Street
Sounded the tread of marching feet;
All day long that free flag tost
Over the heads of the rebel host.

. . . . .

Barbara Frietchie's work is o'er,
And the rebel rides on his raids no more.
Honour to her! and let a tear
Fall, for her sake, on Stonewall's bier."

. . . . .

The house has been pulled down in which Dame Barbara lived, but the incident is remembered by some of the people to whom I spoke. Towards evening I again took the cars, and in rain and darkness reached Emmitsburg, an out-of-the-way small manufacturing town, within a couple of miles of the northern boundary of the State of Maryland. A lumbering old vehicle, which served as omnibus, met us at the railway station and brought us to a primitive hostelry. The coloured man who acted as conductor was also butler, waiter, in short factotum. We, that is a fellow-passenger and myself, along with the household, all supped together at a long table in a kind of general guests' room. The supper, which, in response to my fellow-traveller's inquiries, our coloured friend of the omnibus had dilated on in glowing terms, was very meagre, and I went despondingly to bed. It brought to my mind an old rambling roadside inn I had stopped at some thirty years before in an unfrequented part of Northamptonshire, where the people looked with suspicion and distrust upon all strangers. The next morning I took my place in the ordinary stage, a rude four-wheeled cart, drawn by a pair of horses, and was fortunate in having as my only fellow-passenger a pretty lass of about twenty, "the Maryland rose" as I playfully called her before we parted. The driver, who was also proprietor of the stage, was an intelligent man, full of anecdote, not slow to impart his knowledge of the country, and with a geniality in his grey eye which often brightened as the talk between my fair companion and himself warmed into smart repartee. There is a large convent at Emmitsburg, and many Roman Catholics. Our journey was soon over—only about twelve miles, along a broad country road, over which seventeen years ago divisions of the Federal army had marched to oppose the Confederates, at that time making their great raid into Pennsylvania under Lee.

The small town of Gettysburg nestles in the shadow of a ridge of hills of irregular contour and broken outline, and is the centre of a well-cultivated and rich agricultural district. But for the famous battle fought there the town would probably have remained for ever an obscure country place. Now it is visited by thousands of people and from all nations. You take a buggy and pair of horses in order to see over the battlefield, and I had the good fortune to have as driver and guide a man who was in Gettysburg during the fight, and who was over the ground frequently directly after the battles. The position of the Federals after they were driven through the town on the first day was one of great strength. The extreme right was at Culps Hill, a lump of ground, well wooded, like Alderley, though less steep. Next come Cemetery Hill and ridge, where there was much heavy fighting, then the centre, which occupied a lower level, yet still high ground, and well protected by strong stone breastworks, hastily thrown up; whilst beyond, forming the extreme left of the position, are two hills, named respectively "Little Round Top" and "Round Top" proper.

Draper has well compared the shape of the lines of the Union army to a fishhook, the barb being on their right at Culps Hill; or it may be likened to a horsewhip, bent inwards at the lash end. The

Federal army presented a front of more than three miles long. The Confederates, posted along Seminary ridge and well sheltered by thick woods, occupied a more extended line. The head-quarters of Lee were at the Seminary, a large building, giving a name to the ground, and occupying a position which commands a view of the whole field of battle. The Emmitsburg road, along which I drove into Gettysburg, runs along the valley between the positions held by the two armies. Mead's head-quarters, a wretched little farm, were behind the centre of his line.

During the long days of the 2nd and 3rd July, 1863, these armies of 80,000 men each from the positions described poured death upon one another, making a mighty war cloud that veiled the summer sun. My guide told me that of the inhabitants who remained in the town, after the first day's fighting, when the Confederates occupied the place and requisitioned every morsel of food they could lay hands on, many were huddled together in the cellars, where they heard with terror the constant booming of cannon, the yells of the rebels, the cheers of the Federals, the rattle of musketry, and the crashing of shot and shells, which made a pandemonium of one of the fairest places upon earth. For, standing where the Federal batteries on Cemetery Hill were placed, the eye ranges over a vast expanse of undulating pastoral country, with blue mountains in the background—here and there windmill, tower, or village nestling amidst green and gold, at our feet the busy little town, and behind us the thickly-wooded crags.

At Gettysburg the tide of war which for the second time had surged into the North was rolled back, never more to return. The losses on both sides were truly fearful. Out of 160,000 men engaged 8,000 were killed on the field, 36,000 wounded, many of which number afterwards died in hospital, and 15,000 were missing; a total of 23,000 Federals and 36,000 Confederates.

Here, on Cemetery Hill, the nation has placed a soldiers' memorial, and round about are the graves of three thousand six hundred of her bravest sons. There, are twelve hundred who belonged to New York State; here, eight hundred from Pennsylvania—each State has its separate mound of sorrow. Still more sad, here, too, are the bodies of eight hundred, unknown. Never have I experienced more sorrowful a time than that I passed at these soldiers' graves at Gettysburg. Here, too, upon the occasion of the dedication of this place to its solemn uses, in the presence of a sympathizing crowd of American citizens from all parts of the Union, were uttered those memorable words of Abraham Lincoln, which are now placed upon the marble monument, and which will be remembered to the latest days: "It is for us, the living, rather to dedicate ourselves to the unfinished work which they who fought here have thus far so nobly advanced; to consecrate ourselves to the great task remaining, and to gather from the graves of these honoured dead increased devotion to that cause for which they gave their lives. Here let us resolve that they shall not have died in vain; that this nation shall, under God, have a new birth of freedom; and that government of the people, by the people, and for the people shall not perish forever from the earth."

IX. COLUMBIA, HARRISBURG, BUFFALO, AND NIAGARA.

LEFT Gettysburg in a very sober frame of mind, taking the train for Harrisburg, the capital of Pennsylvania, by way of Columbia. The country generally through which we travelled was well cultivated, with a considerable population, evidently in a comfortable condition. Everybody seems to be prosperous. At Columbia the railway crosses the Susquehanna river by an iron bridge more than a mile in length. It is a busy, thriving place; the streets at right angles, as usual; there is a fine opera-house and numerous hotels. I had only half an hour in the place, and was recommended by the railway clerk to get a cup of tea at the restaurant close by, kept by one John Warren, a coloured man. It was excellent tea, nicely put before me, for five cents!

The railway from Columbia runs alongside the Susquehanna, the most picturesque river I had yet seen, wide and shallow, tumbling over its rocky bed and splashing its way to the far-off sea. Lofty wood-clad hills are on each side, now coloured with many hues and burnished with the glory of the setting sun. The cars are well filled, and at every station considerable numbers come in and go out. It is clearly a well-used, paying route. It seemed to me very like the Yorkshire or East Lancashire of America.

At Harrisburg, where I arrived in time for a late dinner, there was a grand demonstration in progress by the Republican party, and I had another opportunity of seeing a torchlight procession, of which our cousins appear to be very fond. Some of the uniforms of these torch-bearers are quite grotesque. But what struck me most was the seriousness, I might say earnestness, with which the whole procession business is carried on. The State House and grounds here are imposing, and, as in most of the older towns, the trees are a pleasing feature. There is here, too, a magnificent soldiers' monument— a simple colossal obelisk, placed in the centre of a square where four streets meet, the most impressive monument I had seen.

I was stirring early the next morning, and caught the train at 4·30 to Williamsport and Watkins Glen. One of the towns we passed about daylight, Milton, had been burnt down during the summer, and it was curious to see the sweep a fire makes in a town built mainly of wood. The streets are mapped out by the few charred outlines left near the ground, with now and then the outer shell of a large brick building standing alone.

We continue to run alongside the beautiful Susquehanna, through Williamsport, where excellent fare awaits the hungry traveller, and comfortable time for his refreshment is also allowed him. The railways are clearly made for the convenience of travellers here, and not merely to give the minimum of comfort. It is quite true that the long distances to be got over in the States force the railway people to consider the requirements and conveniences of passengers more than with us in England; there are various matters not absolutely necessary on our shorter journeys, but which, if provided, would save worlds of discomfort. Look at any large station—what a rush there is in certain directions after a run of an hour or two! I do not mean to say that in American railway cars there are no discomforts, for I have travelled sixteen or eighteen hours at a spell in a smoking carriage, and the occasional sweepings-out were not agreeable to witness. But even the vile habit of spitting is, I am informed, much less general than in earlier days.

At Elmira I was joined by some American friends, at whose suggestion I visited Watkins Glen, in a picturesque part of the country, through which the Northern Central Railway runs on the way to Buffalo and Niagara Falls. Watkins Glen is of the character of the gorge of Pfeffers, at Ragatz, in Switzerland. You enter at the lowest end between two high rocks, which have probably been cut through by the action of water wearing incessantly for ages past. A stream of considerable volume and power now rushes through the glen, which is some miles long, making some pretty cascades and waterfalls; it abounds in deliciously-cool pools, moss-grown and lichen-stained rocks, and fantastic paths. Across the chasm, near the head of the glen, is thrown a railway bridge, light and elegant in structure, and sufficiently in the air to try the nerves of the timid as the train rolls across. At the time of my visit the trees were a special feature, bright with October hues. From the hotel balcony at Watkins one has a grand view of the extended valley into which the waters of the various glens fall, and at the lower end of the valley is Lake Seneca, upon which steamers ply to Geneva, a town at the head of the lake.

By the warm fireside of the excellent hotel at Corning, for the weather had gone suddenly very cold, we dined and waited for our train, which in the evening carried us along to Buffalo. I was out in the streets in the early morning, and came suddenly upon a view of Lake Erie, dotted with the white sails of ships. Buffalo, built upon the extreme easterly end of Lake Erie during the present century, contains a large population, with fine, wide, business streets, and tree-lined avenues in the suburbs, stretching away towards the country; altogether an important place, quite realizing both in extent, activity, and picturesqueness the title it holds of Queen City of the Lakes. Fruit from the Far West in plenty is on sale on the sidewalks opposite the fruiterers' stores, and in the great thoroughfares are streams of busy people intent upon the almighty dollar. But upon this bright morning my eye continually wanders beyond the fringe of shipping, which hugs the town, so to speak, to the far-stretching expanse of water, Lake Erie. We walk in this direction, past the fort and military station, towards that narrowing neck of water which becomes Niagara River. By-and-by we take the train through flat country; but the novelty of seeing immense peach orchards as we move along, combined with a strong undercurrent of expectancy, make that short railway ride of twenty miles or so anything but dull. At length our train is gliding over a light iron suspension bridge, which, at a height of more than two hundred feet, spans the Niagara River. Down below, between the clean-cut rocks on either side, the water rushes and foams. Before we have crossed the stream the eye for a moment rests upon the mighty cataract, with the pictures of which it has long been familiar, and we feel that we have just seen Niagara Falls.

We stay on the Canadian side, at the Clifton House, to which we drive along the river bank; and on the verandah, outside our rooms, we sit and watch and wonder at the scene. The sun is shining brilliantly, and there is only a slight motion in the air; yet a delicate film of gossamer spray is wafted towards us, and looking through it, across the river chasm, we see in front of the sounding cataract, painted in bright colours, a rainbow, quivering, as it seems, under the sun's bright rays. I walked along the Canadian side, towards the horse-shoe fall; there seems to be an irresistible power of attraction in the deep bass-toned thunder, steadily beating time. Here one realizes Goethe's expression, "unhasting yet unresting." The air is filled with sound, not loud—subdued, melodious, almost articulate in its wonderful fascination. It takes time, after being set down here, to apprehend the relations of your surroundings; to find out, in fact, where you are. You are told that the river here is about 5,000 feet wide, measuring from the American fall and round the horse-shoe fall to the Canadian shore. Also that the falls are only one hundred and sixty feet or so. Then you are beset by an eager crowd of people who are desirous of showing you this, that, and the other thing, for which you have only to pay a dollar or two. Every conceivable pretext is used for vulgarizing the place and taking money out of your pocket unnecessarily. This is beyond all others the place at which travellers require this warning. After some hours you free yourself, and are more at liberty to sit down quietly and stare. This may sound strange, but I repeat here you must look for a long time upon the wonders before you in order that you may help yourself to see truly. Few who watch that ceaseless rush at Niagara realize that through this narrow channel the waters of four inland seas, draining a surface equal to the continent of Europe, pour their overflow into Ontario and along the majestic St. Lawrence to the sea. From the remote regions of Lake Superior, the picturesque Huron, the ocean-like Michigan, and the busy Erie, comes unceasingly this resistless torrent which has during uncounted ages cut the rock channel of Niagara river for more than twenty miles. Look how majestically the mass of water moves over the rocky ledge; in times of autumnal drought, as when I saw the fall, that gliding mass is sixteen feet of solid water as it goes over for the plunge; in rainy seasons it is more than twenty feet thick. And what magnificent colour! As the mass of water slides down to the abyss, a broad band of wonderful green is disclosed, beautiful in its translucence as the rainbows which play perpetually near. I am giving these details so that those at home may be helped to create a picture of this wonderful cataract. My first impression was the grandeur of the sound; next, what I may call the rhythmical roll of the vast watery mass, which holds you, as I said before, fascinated. But look how, out of the deep hurly-burly down below, where the gigantic blows fall unceasingly, arises the steaming spray. You have seen this cloud, low hanging near the ground, from afar, and knew that there was Niagara; but watch, now you are near, the mighty wreath, how it rises higher and higher, the most wonderful fountain on the earth, until, right at the zenith, you see the last supreme vibration, which shakes off even in its birth a sunlit cloud, that floats away whilst you are gazing. Always changing, but ever with upward whirl, this column of spray is continually weaving clouds that ascend and sail away. We cross to Goat Island, that place of delicious reverie, and watch the waters as they are drawn towards the abyss. In the narrow rocky passages, through which the water plunges and foams, it is not difficult to estimate the enormous forces at work. Within the distance of a mile from the Falls nothing can withstand the mighty downward pulling of this wide swiftly-flowing river.

It is difficult, in analyzing one's feelings, to say whether the fast-flowing stream, before the plunge, broken on its way by Goat Island and various rocks, or the mighty cataract itself is the more impressive. We stand upon the verge of the great Fall—ingenuity has devised safe methods—and gaze upon the roaring waters woven into a thousand forms in their curved descent. Then we watch the boiling flood below, and the eye follows the affrighted stream as it rushes along beneath the light bridge suspended high in air from shore to shore, and the stronger but still slight-looking bridge over which run the railway cars. Then we slowly retrace our steps and come to the American Fall, and after long looking prepare to follow a stalwart guide under the Falls to the Cave of the Winds. No experience can better convey the sense of power than this short walk of some yards under the American Fall at Niagara.

As you approach the Fall from the dressing-house, where you are enveloped in flannels and oilskins, and scramble over and along the rocks and prepared wooden way, you are met with blinding showers of spray, through which you push along. After pausing for a minute or two to breathe and look around, you are under the arch made by the mass of falling water, in a gale of wind; the rain is now heavier, the wind in a fury, and you stand back a few inches in a cleft of the rock, your trusted guide close by; then you go on once more into a storm of redoubled—ay, quadrupled—force; the rain comes upon you as if it meant to kill you by sheer force of pelting, hard hits upon your face and head and body tell you that you are in a perfect hurricane of wind and rain and eccentric storm—overpowering, unique, sublime. There you feel the power of Niagara, and yet you have only touched the hem of its garment, for as you stand on the narrow ledge of rock, battered by this terrific hurricane, right before you, and through which you see the sunlight, is the vast wall of water, ever falling, ceaseless as Time.

I do not know anything that has so much impressed me with a sense of the sublime as Niagara Falls. In crossing the Atlantic, as I have already related, a new world was revealed, and, if I may venture to say so, an increased power of spiritual vision obtained. Here, too, the same faculties of imaginative sympathy were stirred, and I felt that the voice of Niagara was at one with the earth's rotation and the movements of the stars.

X. CLEVELAND AND CHICAGO.

WHEN I started from the Clifton House rainbows were playing on the face of Niagara, and around the base of that wonderful column of spray which rises out of the boiling gulf below the Falls. I was sorry to have to leave this wonderful cataract, and those American friends who had been my companions there. The train rapidly carried me to Buffalo, and then along the south shore of Lake Erie, through unexciting farming country, by orchards of ten thousand peach trees, by pretty villages, and now and then into a busy town.

It was night when I reached my destination, still on the shore of Lake Erie, at Cleveland, Ohio, where I found a most excellent hostelry, the Kennard House, with unexceptionable fare. The Forest city, as Cleveland is called, is considered by many Americans to be the most beautiful city in the Union, and it has many advantages, being on the shore of a great lake and surrounded by finely wooded country. Cleveland is built on both banks of the Cuyahoga river, and is a very busy place, its manufactories making such a valley of smoke as we see at Stockport or Sheffield. Once out of the river valley, however, the city is clean, with wide streets and squares, and far-stretching, well-wooded avenues, on each side of which are detached houses with abundant lawns and greenery, not fenced, but for the most part quite open to the street.

I had an opportunity of sitting awhile in court with an eminent Judge on the last day for the registration of voters, and the crowd was not of a character generally to raise one's estimate of democracy. Many were clearly recent importations from Europe, and not a few were Irish. I happened in my rambles about the town to come upon the Democratic electors' head-quarters for Cleveland, and the score or so of hangers on there were certainly as rough-looking a lot of fellows as the most rampant Jingoism could desire. During my stay in Cleveland there was a great Republican demonstration; in the procession were at least two thousand five hundred men on horseback, many thousands on foot, bands of music at short intervals, and flags and banners in profusion. Euclid Avenue and Superior Street are the two chief arteries through which fashion and business circulate.

I left Cleveland in the evening, taking the sleeping cars to Chicago, which city I reached in time for breakfast at the Grand Pacific, one of the busiest and most complete hotels in the States. Chicago, situated at the south-west corner of the shore of Lake Michigan, on the river Chicago, is a wonderful growth. Fifty years ago the place consisted of a few huts and a dozen families, besides the garrison of the United States Fort there. About the time that Manchester obtained its Charter of Incorporation, Chicago had been incorporated a year, and had a population under five thousand. It has a population now of about six hundred thousand. General Grant told a friend of mine in New York that when he was a boy his father lived west and kept a pony for him, that he (the General) had often ridden over the site of Chicago, and that he had no doubt the land then could have been bought for the value of his pony—fifteen dollars, Sir! The Chicago of to-day has been built since the year 1871, when the great fire consumed several square miles of property.

The city is laid out rectangularly, the streets running east and west, the avenues north and south. These avenues are miles long—the first friend upon whom I called lived at 2,802, Prairie Avenue, and another at 3,741, Vincennes. Tramcars run everywhere. The Post Office and the Court House are magnificent buildings. I could not help thinking of Manchester, with her wretched dingy hole of a Post Office, and the twenty years' delay and loss of time and money by the Government in preparing plans for a new building.

I was fortunate in being in Chicago on a Sunday in lovely October weather, so that I saw the people in holiday dress. Nothing in the towns I visited pleased me more than the Parks of Chicago. Their existence shows markedly the forethought and consideration for the welfare of the people which has been exercised by those who have the conduct of affairs. The Lincoln Park, of great extent along the shore of Lake Michigan, contains also a zoological garden, and affords an agreeable and refreshing change to tens of thousands of the people, to whom it belongs. There are no entrance gates or railed enclosure; the park is always freely open to all. South Park is distant about six miles from the centre of the city, and is a grand expanse of woodland country, laid out in carriage drives and walks. Although so far away, avenues stretch to it from the city, and no doubt in a very few years the city will have grown much nearer to the park. Besides these two parks, which are on the east, looking over the great inland sea, there are on the west the Douglas Park, the Central Park, and the Humboldt Park, laid out on a great scale, and connected by broad boulevards. The times will come, most likely during the lives of the present younger generation, when the city of Chicago will be the foremost city of the American continent, for there the east and west join hands, and through Chicago is poured a stream of timber, corn, beef, mutton, pork, and the fruits of the earth, such as the world has never before seen. Numerous corn elevators stand up against the clear sky, like vast, stranded Noah's arks. These elevators are very large warehouses, fitted up with exquisite machinery for the manipulation of grain, loading and unloading with despatch vast quantities. The storage capacity of the Chicago elevators is said to be twenty millions of bushels of grain.

One of the chief sights and wonders of this city of yesterday is the Union stock yards, where the droves of live stock are sorted and sold. You take a tramcar which runs in an hour to the centre of the cattle pens, and near which are built huge warehouses, in which the killing of oxen and swine, and preserving the meat, is carried on. I went to the largest of these pig-killing places, where they told me that in the busy season they can kill 13,000 pigs daily. It is a horrible sight—the squeaking of the brutes rings in my ears now—and I should recommend everybody not to see it. The swine are driven from the pens along the platform, which runs into the main building. Here about a dozen at a time reach the last pen, in which a man is stationed, who seizes a pig and hooks to one of its hind legs a chain. It is instantly pulled up, suspended over a huge vat, and is pushed forward along a beam about a yard, when a man with a sharp knife pierces the throat, and it is all over directly. This goes on incessantly like clock-work. The pigs slide along and are next scalded and scraped. The interior is taken out. The feet and head are cut off, the hams and hands and the flitches separated, and the various parts are then passed to the salting cellar and refrigerator, where they are in due time sent forth for consumption. The cattle pens occupy, I judge, several hundred acres of land.

Next to these the vast stores of timber you see piled on this side of the city astonished me. It is said that the largest timber trade in the world is done at Chicago. The lumber yards are on the south branch of Chicago river about two miles from the cattle yards. The Chicago river not more than a mile near its outlet into the lake makes a harbour for shipping of the largest size—running almost straight through the centre of the city—then it forks north and south, the southern branch giving water way to the lumber and stock yards.

The people of Chicago are justly proud of their waterworks. The chief supply is from Lake Michigan; they have also a number of Artesian wells. The engines at the waterworks have a pumping power of over seventy millions of gallons a day.

It is a delightful experience to sit in a buggy, behind a pair of good horses and to drive along the avenues or boulevards of this great city, looking out upon the green waters of Lake Michigan, that stretches like ocean, beyond the distant horizon. The air is fresh, the sky clear, the trees brown, and yellow, and red, the vast lake lively with white-sailed ships; a far off thin line of smoke tells of a distant steamer; here about us are the busy crowds of people, joyous under the influence of this brilliant sunlight.

I spent the evening of this day at the house of my friend, Brooke Herford, where I met Tom Hughes, just back from his newly-founded colony, Rugby, in Tennessee. Years before he had suggested and originated a free library in Chicago, and only yesterday had been fêted, and been shown how his small beginning had developed into a magnificent collection of over sixty thousand volumes, which are doing their work well.

In the morning hours I had a last walk about the city. The numerous bridges over the Chicago river, the many vessels of varied descriptions which crowd the stream, the busy, wide streets of the trading quarter of the city, State Street and Madison Street especially; Wabath, and Michigan, and Prairie Avenues, with their thousands of beautiful residences, each with its plot of garden ground, and all along graced with the foliage of forest trees; these deepened my impressions, and made a picture to which delighted memory clings.

Never did I feel more reluctant to turn back on a journey than at Chicago, for this was the most westerly point of my too hurried travels, and I remembered how Longfellow had kindly said to my friend from Rhode Island, "Be sure that you do not let him go back to England without seeing a prairie!" And now I had to turn my face eastward without this experience. Another friend, too, who had long lived out in the region round Lake Superior, said to me that in the early summer time when the grasses and flowers were in their prime, it would be impossible to describe the extraordinary wealth of delicate odours which filled the air on the prairies of the far west.

XI. CANADA AND THE LAKES.

ON the afternoon of an October day, full of the beauty of colour on land and sea and sky, I drove for the last time along the streets of Chicago to the railway depôt. Baskets of delicious fruit from California were strewn around; I bought peaches, pears, apples, and grapes enough for a pleasant refreshment for four of us, all for seventy-five cents, basket included! At length we are moving off, for some miles in sight of Lake Michigan, and as evening came on through undulating country. We were on board a sleeping car, and had as part of our train a palace dining saloon. At supper time I refreshed, at a cost of seventy-five cents. Here is the bill of fare:—

MICHIGAN CENTRAL DINING CAR.
Supper Bill of Fare.

Oolong Tea.   Coffee.   Iced Tea.

BREAD.

French Loaf.   Boston Brown Bread.   Hot Biscuit.
Dry Dipped and Buttered Toast.

BROILED.

Tenderloin Steak, plain.
,,   with mushroom or tomato sauce.
Sugar Cured Ham.   Sirloin Steak.
Mutton Chops, plain and with tomato sauce.
Lake Michigan White Fish.

GAME.

Broiled Pigeon.

OYSTERS.

Raw.   Stewed.
Boston Baked Beans.

EGGS.

Boiled.   Scrambled.   Fried.
Omelet, plain or with jelly.

COLD DISHES.

Tongue.   Ham.   Beef.   Sardines.

VEGETABLES.

Fried Potatoes, stewed, boiled, and sweet.

RELISHES.

Chow Chow.   Olives.   Currant Jelly.
Mixed Pickles.   Sweet Pickles.
Beet Root.   Celery.   French Mustard.

DESSERT.

Assorted Cake.   Brevoort Ice Cream.
Fruits in Season.

Champagne, Clarets, Sauternes, Ales, Porters, etc.,
can be had on board at the usual prices.

We had a merry time of it over the supper and for an hour or two before bed-time, which is usually very early on board a train, most people beginning to wish for sleep by nine o'clock or so. The next morning we were at Hamilton by about six o'clock, where we had to leave our luxurious train, which goes on to New York. There was sufficient light as we neared Hamilton to see that the character of the country had changed considerably since we saw the sun go down the previous night. Rocky, broken country, with long patches of cultivation, old-fashioned farmsteads, and now and then large villages, came into view, and there was an indefinable something which made us think of home. Probably it was the simple fact, which showed itself in many ways, that we were in an older settled country than that we had so recently left. There was not time at Hamilton to see the town, but its surroundings are pleasant. Soon we were in the train again, moving on a single line through farming lands often fringed at no great distance with clumps of pine forest. Shortly we came in sight of Lake Ontario, and quickly ran into the station at Toronto. Here my stay was short, my chief object being to call upon various friends, among whom was one of whom I feel that his leaving us was a public loss to England—I mean Goldwin Smith, who is settled happily in Toronto, in a charming house with delightful surroundings; and although he must be doing good work in Canada, he can be ill spared by the old country. We spent a pleasant hour or two together, and after a run through the town, the suburbs, and the picturesque park which surrounds the University, and a look in at the courts, I made my way to the steamer *Spartan* on Lake Ontario.

Toronto has a most attractive appearance from the water; rising gradually from the shore and intermingled with much foliage, are many church spires and towers of various kinds, which, combined with the masts of shipping about the wharves and the waters of the Lake, make a bright picture. The sail on Lake Ontario is very like going to sea, as the Lake is something like two hundred miles long and fifty miles across. The steamer is well appointed, the table well supplied with excellent plain food, and the captain a most genial host. It is morning before we reach Kingston, a dull town, straggling along the Lake bank, where we take on passengers. Shortly after leaving here we are steaming down the river St. Lawrence and threading our way through the Thousand Islands, many of them covered with trees, now in rich autumn colours; by-and-by we are shooting the rapids of Long Sault, nine miles in length, down which we rush at high speed, although carried only by the strength of the current. The descent lasts long enough to become exhilarating, and to many people exciting. The St. Lawrence is a magnificent wide-sweeping river, grand by its breadth of water, but the banks do not impress one, never rising beyond quiet beauty, and often tame.

We have another night of innocent festivity on board the steamer, and about seven in the morning we touch the quay at Montreal, and make for the Windsor Hotel, one of the largest and at the same time most comfortable houses in America. After breakfast we drive to "the Mountain," an eminence behind the city, covered thickly with forest, but through which excellent carriage roads have been made to the best points of view of the magnificent scene; Montreal at our feet, mapped out quite distinctly, the wide St. Lawrence stretching right and left far as the eye can reach, and crossing the river is the Victoria Tubular Bridge, a mile and three-quarters long, one of the engineering wonders of the world.

Montreal is a fine city, full of commercial activity and with abundant attractions to lovers of the picturesque. For myself the river and the shipping are sights sufficient; but besides these I spent a good part of the day in what we call in Lancashire "mooning" about the crowded streets of interesting shops or stores. Here, as in all other places I had been, were warm-hearted friends ready to make my visit a happy one; and here, too, I met, as elsewhere, faces and names from the old country, to whom tidings from our common home were a delight. It is a happy circumstance, that all over that Northern Continent of America are people who not only speak the English language, but who have actually in the days gone by gone forth from every county in great Britain and Ireland to make a new home for themselves and their children. These are the links which bind us, and, along with deep intuitions, draw our imaginations continually to the West.

Towards evening I went on board the steamer for Quebec, and with hearty greetings from friends and a good round drink, according to the customs of the place, we parted for a time from Montreal. The sail along the St. Lawrence in October by night is less interesting than it would be under the light of a summer sun or a harvest moon, and as we were not favoured with either, we were driven in upon ourselves and the resources of the steamer for the evening. I spent an hour or two and some dollars in looking over and buying various odds and ends of pretty and ingenious Indian work, and in photographs of several places previously visited. Morning brought us to

Quebec, on a hill or cape rising out of the rivers St. Lawrence and St. Charles, most interesting historically, with more of an old-world aspect than all the cities I had visited on the other side the Atlantic. Curious old streets, clambering along hill-sides; quaint gabled houses nodding to each other across narrow passages; tumbledown low-roofed places; churches, convents, squares with modern shops; steep stair-like alleys, like Clovelly in Devonshire; the great citadel towering over all, and in its shadow the fine sweeping Durham Terrace overlooking the river, the lower town, and the lofty ridge on the other side, dotted with a line of forts and villages and a town, ample materials out of which an artist in words might build up a wonderful and glowing picture. In the upper town is a monument to Wolfe and Montcalm—a plain obelisk set upon a solid base, with a simple inscription to the memory of the two men. Churches abound, both of the older faith and Protestants of all denominations. Hospitals, Convents, Music Hall, Courthouse, City Hall, and University are all interesting. But more than all are we attracted to the monument on the plains of Abraham, where Wolfe nobly fought and conquering fell. During the day we had an enjoyable drive of some dozen miles through old French and Indian villages, to the falls of Montmorenci. It is a lofty waterfall of great beauty. On our return in the evening we took once more to the river, and in the twilight, which soon deepened into night, steamed along the wide, swift-flowing St. Lawrence, now dotted with many lights, in the direction of Montreal.

We had the disagreeable experience of a dense fog in the river St. Lawrence on this return voyage to Montreal, than which nothing is more uncomfortable. You can neither go on properly nor stand still, and there is constant danger. After much wearisome delay we made our port, a few hours late. In the afternoon, after seeing the fine cemetery of Mount Royal, on the slope of Montreal Mountain, and very beautiful, I took the train running by Lake Champlain, a grand expanse of water, with most attractive rocky shore: in the summer time a favourite resort. I saw it under the light of a young autumnal moon, riding on the platform of the last carriage of our train, the coloured conductor explaining various points of interest as we rattled through the rocky country along the Derbyshire-like curves. Afterwards I availed myself of the comfort of a sleeping car, and awoke in time to catch glimpses of the Hudson River ere we rushed into the Central Railway Terminus in New York City.

I have hitherto said little of the three lakes I had passed, and which form so important a feature of the country. Without doubt Lake Michigan is the grandest of those I saw, although, with the exception of Chicago, Erie has more important cities along its shores. But Michigan, Erie, and Ontario are all vast inland seas, over which the north winds beat, as they do in the Atlantic, driving many a good ship to her destruction. Only the week after I left the shores of Michigan a fine steamer left port one evening and was seen no more. Fragments of her timbers and a few bodies cast upon the beach told the sad story of her end. And yet always the men who have moved west have been attracted to these picturesque shores, Buffalo, Erie, Cleveland, Sandusky, Toledo, and Detroit, round Lake Erie; Hamilton, Toronto, Kingston, Oswego, and Rochester, near Ontario; Grand Haven, Milwaukee, and Chicago, on Lake Michigan—all these and many smaller towns show how the convenience of a water-way, as well as the attraction of beauty, have drawn population round these inland seas. Even the lonely and grand Lake Superior is drawing men to its shores; and in the Dominion, still farther north, from the Red River Settlement and the district of Manitoba, beyond the remote Winnipeg, tidings reach us of a wave of enterprising emigration flowing to that ancient home of the untamed bison and the Red Indian. Wood and water, fuel and drink, are the prime necessaries of man, and these are here in abundance.

XII. THE HUDSON RIVER, NEW YORK, THE VOYAGE HOME.

IT was a clear bright morning, near the end of October, a sharp wind blowing from the north, when I took a tramcar in Twenty-third Street for the quays upon the Hudson River. Here is seen one of the features of this enterprising and well-placed city. For a mile or two along the river bank are wharves built out into the river, from which steamers start to all parts of the world; no matter what size, from the smallest river ferry-boat to the Arizona, the largest ship afloat after the Great Eastern, there is abundant room, with deep water to ride in, and a safe mooring ground. Here the Cunard, the Inman, the White Star, the National, the North German, and other lines of Atlantic steamers are all loading or unloading; as well as many of the great river and coasting vessels, of which I have already given some account. To-day I am taking the opportunity of the last day trip of the season to be made by one of the magnificent New York and Albany river boats, the *Albany*, capable of carrying three thousand people, fitted up like a palace, and going at the rate of from fifteen to twenty miles an hour. There are many hundred passengers on board, attracted by the brilliant morning and the last run of the year.

When we steam away from the quay and are breasting the stream, New York is on our right, and we have the reverse picture of that I described in my voyage along the East river; every spire and tower and block of building is outlined sharply against the sky, the river is busy with quick-darting small steam tugs, with sailing ships, with many river boats, and with the leviathan ferries; there is a fine "snap" in the air, as a lively American girl said to me, which gives an air of cheerfulness to the animated scene, probably the reflection of our own minds. We soon leave Jersey city behind us, but for ten miles up the river extend the city and suburbs of New York ; then we pass Fort Lee on high land on the western side. On both banks of the river are numerous villa residences, those on the Jersey side especially commanding views of New York and the ever-changing stream. By-and-by, we pass on our right the Harlem river, which, running from the Hudson into the East river, completes the belt of water, and makes Manhattan Island, upon which New York is built. On our left are the Palisades of the Hudson, a huge, clean-cut wall of rock, stretching over fifteen miles, and rising occasionally more than five hundred feet above the grand river, not mud-coloured, but of a green tint, flowing quickly through a deep channel almost a mile in breadth. The Tappan Zee and Haverstraw Bay reaches, through which we shall sail, are nearly three miles in width. As we leave the Palisades, upon which at one point is noticeable an immense hotel, the Palisades Mountain House, showing how attractive a resort it is in the hot summer days, we enter the Tappan Reach, passing by the State prison at Sing-Sing, and enter a region of lofty hills, wood-crowned and picturesque. Each turn of the stream reveals new beauties, which culminate as we approach West Point. There I landed, in the most delightful part of the Highlands of the Hudson. West Point, the military school of the United States, is a charming place, and the views from the hotel verandah, looking north up the reach of river running to Newburgh, right before you on the far off hill side, are wonderfully beautiful. Rock and wood and water are here rarely combined, and my impression, vivid as on the day I sailed there, is that the Hudson river surpasses any river I have seen for beauty and grandeur.

I have steamed along this grand river fifty miles, only a third of the distance the Albany will run, and as I stand near the hotel at West Point she steams away in mid-stream, looking at this distance quite a small vessel, so grand are the hills which encircle the sweeping reaches of this majestic river. Standing at old Fort Putnam, just above West Point, the eye wanders over a wide range of hills, covered for the most part with thick wood, brilliant now with colour, varying from 1,400 to nearly 2,000 feet high, around the lower slopes of which the Hudson finds its course. In the days when Hampden and

Cromwell were fighting for liberty in the old country, from which the *Mayflower* sailed to Plymouth rock, over these ranges of high land roamed tribes of red Indians, whose only memorials are to be found in the names they have left behind.

I had a delightful couple of hours of quiet rambling about West Point before crossing by steam ferry to the train, which took me back rapidly, running along the east bank of the Hudson to New York.

The two best places to dine in New York are Delmonico's and the Brunswick Hotel, both in Fifth Avenue. Here you can have everything that the most epicurean palate may desire. On my last evening in New York, we went to the Madison Square theatre, which is peculiarly constructed. The orchestra is above the proscenium, the effect of the music being exceedingly pleasing. There are two stages, so that intervals are very short between acts, set scenes being arranged on one stage, whilst acting is going on on the other. We saw the popular play of *Hazel Kirke*, which was having a long run. The American theatres are all well arranged, and there are few of the inequalities in outward appearance we see at home. There is no dress circle, one of the essential differences of an American indoor crowd and one elsewhere is that the people are all well-dressed and clothed with self-respect, which gives even a serious aspect to an audience. There is little applause in any theatre I was in and no enthusiasm. Between the acts iced water is handed round.

A visit to New York would be incomplete without some notice of the slums and places of amusement of the masses of the people. And I had arranged, with a young fellow-townsman, that before leaving should there be an opportunity, I would make an arrangement with the detective police to be shown those amusements and vices which are to be found in all modern cities. I had on a previous evening spent a pleasant hour at one of the largest music saloons, Koster and Bial's Garden, Twenty-third Street, Sixth Avenue, where it was refreshing to see the crowd of orderly, well-conducted people of both sexes, enjoying the performance of excellent music by a numerous band of musicians. There is no doubt a large consumption of lager beer at this and like places. The large hall, hung with paintings, fitted up with hundreds of chairs and small tables and lighted with the electric light, is an attraction in itself. There is a large German element in the crowd which nightly spends its time and takes supper here.

The Bowery, New York, has always had a notoriety as a rough unsafe region at night for unguarded wayfarers; many murders and other crimes have been done there; and one of the first places to which our intelligent conductor led us, was a dark passage leading to a blind court of three or four large houses, each occupied by many families, all of the lowest class, mostly criminal. The place is called Donovan's Court, from the fact of a murder of unusual horror, by a man of that name, having been perpetrated there. Daylight has been let into many of these dark places during the past few years by city improvements, and by the efforts of self-denying, religious men and women especially.

We next went into what from the street appeared to be an ordinary common beerhouse, but really a sparring crib kept by one Owen Geoghan. Here was an assemblage of men and women of the lowest type I have seen. Drinking and noise in these places go together. Near the inner end of the room was a platform, about three feet from the floor, roped round, and on this presently appeared, two men stripped for an encounter. It was not fighting, as they were gloved, but they hit each other very hard, and were well tired after a few rounds. All this time drinking and noise continue. There are various such places hereabouts.

Next we went for half an hour to Kramer's Atlantic Gardens, so-called—a large German music hall, which at this hour, about midnight, is filled with many hundreds of men, women, and young people. To the table next to that at which we sat came two families and had supper, chiefly German sausage in quantity and lager beer. This is a respectable place of amusement. Our guide told me that he came here occasionally, bringing his wife and any of her friends; and it is quite unique, for the band of musicians consists of women performers, chiefly on stringed instruments. The ladies' orchestra was a novelty to us; they played excellently various pieces from Gounod, Mozart, Auber, and Strauss. On Sunday sometimes as many as two thousand five hundred people go there, the average being sixteen hundred.

About forty barrels of lager beer are consumed on one of these occasions. But a Teuton will sit all night long with a mug of lager before him listening to the music and smoking the inevitable pipe.

Our next turn took us to the saddest sight I saw, the lowest places in Water Street into which seamen and others are enticed by women who have gradually sunk down to this lowest hell in human life. We went into two places, the "Caledonian Hall" and "The Man at the Wheel," both low drinking houses and dancing shops opening on to the street. Here truly might be written up the most tragic words of Dante, "Abandon hope, all ye that enter!" To my surprise I found that one of these places was kept by a Salford woman, who, on learning we were from her neighbourhood, wished us in true Lancashire fashion to have something to drink.

Our next visit was to a Chinese opium smoking place, in a cellar, where Chinamen and others who wish inhale the deadly intoxicant. Our stay here was not long, and none but Chinamen were there, but I saw enough to feel the truth of Dickens's descriptions in Edwin Drood, and was glad when we left the den. Then we came to a street in which most doors were open, and where, out of each house, through crimson curtains, came light and laughter; of which Solomon said long ago, "The end of that mirth is heaviness, for he knoweth not that the dead are there; and that her guests are in the depths of hell." It would be hard to describe what we witnessed in the houses we visited here—but I will say that we saw both white and coloured humanity under circumstances which show how unaltered is human nature for several thousands of years. Alas! it was a night of sorrowful memories; what tragic histories had I not read in the faces of some of those who had passed before us, and I felt how impotent and imperfect in some directions is our much-vaunted civilization. It is the saddest side of our modern life, only to be changed by ages of suffering and woe.

The night was wearing fast, so driving through the almost deserted streets, we moved towards the river, and shortly reached the Cunard wharf, where I said good-bye to my young townsman and tried to find an hour's sleep. I was stirring early, for various friends had come to say farewell; punctually to the hour of starting, six o'clock a.m., preparations were astir for casting off, and in fifteen minutes we felt the vibrations of our propelling machinery and were soon moving down the Hudson. It is a melancholy scene in the early morning in October, cold and wet; and after the start we were all very quiet for a time. By-and-by, as the great sun rushed up over the sea, making the sky aflame with light, we became more cheerful, and as we looked around and saw the scenes we had looked upon as we neared America a month ago, some among us brightened up and laid ourselves out for a pleasant time.

We had on board the *Bothnia* about one hundred and seventy cabin passengers and about forty forward. It takes a day or two to settle down in your quarters and to find out who are to be your companions during the voyage. We had not, however, been at sea forty-eight hours before it looked like troubled water, and a goodly number of our friends preferred to remain on deck when the bell rung at meal times. Then we got into roughish weather, and the racks were put on the tables, the attendance thereat becoming "small by degrees and beautifully less." Fortunately, I escaped all feeling of uneasiness, and was able thoroughly to enjoy the changing scene. How unlike our outward voyage. One comfort there was, however, we had no fog; but heavy rain now and then and a rolling, tossing sea, that gave the troubled voyager little rest. After we had been out a week or so it became a matter of calculation whether we should be in port by Saturday night. We had hoped at the start to reach England on Saturday morning, then as the run on the day showed under two hundred miles, hope gave way to despondency, and Sunday night or Monday morning was the time looked for.

It was a magnificent sight to watch from the deck the rolling of the mighty Atlantic waves, first as they came on steadily in front, the vessel rising on the waves; then as we passed over and descended into the deep valley between each roller, to see the mighty wall of water rise up like a mountain behind us and slide away. Hour after hour have I watched and wondered at these gigantic waves as they rolled along; now and then, as if by some freak, instead of rising as it neared the wave our good ship would put its prow right into the water; then came a mighty rushing whirl and a scampering out of the way by passengers; two or three feet of solid water rushing along is not to be trifled with. Then we should get a blow sideways from some eccentric wave, and the ship would shudder, as it were, and seemed to be struck motionless for a moment, ere she plunged forward once more, riding upon the waves. And so we went on for days and nights, when it was dark, for the moon had died away after the first night or two. The stars were at times very bright. I saw several of the moons of Jupiter through my ordinary opera glass. At length the weather moderated, not that we had experienced any heavy winds, for we were told that the winds we had experienced did not account for the heavy sea—the wind was, fortunately for us, elsewhere.

It is impossible to give a complete idea of the wonderful effect a change of weather from cold and stormy to sunshine and a smoother sea has upon a couple of hundred people on board an Atlantic steamer. Yesterday and as I have said for seven or eight days past, invalids have been below or reclining on deck in chairs under heavy wrappers, having their slight needs brought up to them and undergoing a perpetual process of coddling. Now and then a shower of rain would come and flutter the crowd of sufferers, and then patience would give way under the small trial. Occasionally a sail was seen at some distance, and a slight sensation of tidings from afar would stir the ship. Then we should watch for her signals and our return message, and again the wide waste of waters would present no object upon which the eye could rest. Several times upon our voyage large shoals of porpoises would leap along with the ship, and now and then a solitary bird fluttered as if exhausted and rested awhile upon the rigging of our mainmast. The jollier, stronger section of the passengers would between meals, which seemed to come often, amuse themselves by whist, poker, euchre, and other games at cards, or playing at sea quoits or sea skittles, or getting up auctions or pools, or singing in the smoke-room, or gathering in a knot would discuss some vexed question in politics or ecclesiastical affairs. To-day the pure air and wonderful sky of cloudless blue has diffused not only an invigorating influence over the passengers externally, but there seems to be a purer moral atmosphere. Books are more in request, letter-writing is resumed, conversations more æsthetical than polemical are the order of the day.

During the voyage we have made the acquaintance of various officers of the ship, and the chief engineer, Mr. Brown, a capital fiddler, suggests that, with so much musical talent on board, we might get up a concert. Consider it done, Mr. Brown, was our reply, and accordingly steps were taken, and—having obtained the captain's consent—the entertainment organised. A collection had been made on the previous Sunday, after a sermon by the Bishop of Edinburgh, when the sum of £19 was collected. To-night, Friday, we intend to make another effort to supplement this sum in aid of the Seaman's Orphan Hospital at Liverpool. We request four of the most charming girls on the ship to take charge of the collecting, and we have our concert, a Mr. Pim in the chair. We have a prologue written for the occasion by an enthusiastic passenger, and an excellent speech from the chair, and a feeling of peace and goodwill pervades the assembly. The concert is a success, and the collection amounts to £115. Then the more robust, if not the more musical of the party, adjourn to the smoking-room and hold a second or more secular concert until a late hour, and the skies look down smilingly.

The effort to be of use has not been in vain, and the numerous family with the cheerful Captain as our head, in this floating home, is animated with kindlier feeling and with widened human sympathy as we get towards the end of our voyage.

We are nearing land; a little bird flutters on to the ship, and is easily taken by the hand of a sailor, who tenderly cares for it. Shortly before three a.m. it is very dark, a light flashes in the sky, low hanging near the horizon. As we move forward it seems to rise and to come nearer; and by-and-by we resolve the star into, and are passing, the Fastnet Light. Out there, not far beyond, just visible, is a low, black line of rocky coast. It is Ireland! I go down to bed, much pleased with what I have just seen. No other passenger astir. Towards seven o'clock we are nearing Queenstown, and everybody is on deck. Shortly we put in towards the harbour, but only stand off a short time whilst the letter-bags are put on the tender and one or two passengers leave us. Then, as we stand out to sea again, we see the steamship *Gallia*, from Liverpool yesterday, nearing us, and we put off a boat to take their pilot on board our ship. For a few moments we are near each other, and give a grand uplifted shout of welcome.

Presently the pilot comes on board, our engines move, and we are making up Channel; the snow-topped mountains of Ireland telling us the reason of the cold wind which has been blowing for some hours. And so until night we steam towards the Mersey, at the mouth of which river we hang about until next morning, when we sail up between her brown low shores, everything looking as if it had been ink-washed, everybody full of excitement as we near Liverpool. Ah! there is our tender coming! That with the red funnel. Now we look through our glasses for the faces we know so well. Yes, there they are, coming to meet us, God bless them! They are here! It is a time of quiet emotion this returning home, to one's kindred, to Old England, after the perils of the deep. And it is still true, as of old, that "they who go down to the sea in ships see great wonders."

We are on shore; on English ground once more; after the usual Custom-house botheration and cordial farewells to our companions on the sea, we soon reach our train, and by afternoon on Monday, the first of November, are in the old house at home.

XIII. EPILOGUE.

HAD purposed stopping at the end of letter twelve, but there is so much more to be told about what I saw in America, that it may be well to give a baker's dozen of letters, and bring together some generalizations which may interest those who have followed my steps week by week. One prominent fact must occur to all who have traced my wanderings on the map—the great extent of country over which I travelled in four weeks. America is so large that facilities for comfortable travelling are necessarily studied and arranged in a much more complete manner than on this side the water. As I have related, not only sleeping cars but dining cars are attached to the long-distance trains, and where they are not abundant time and provision is made at some convenient station for refreshment. The advantages, too, of the long-carriage system, which affords the means of walking from end to end of the train, are found out in these long journeys. There is also usually "on board" a large collection of books and periodicals for sale. In all the trains I entered, and they were many, iced water was placed in every carriage or brought round by a boy at intervals. And in almost every carriage was a ladies' or gentlemen's lavatory. On the river steamers and the boats which run along the Sound the same careful provision for the comforts of passengers is shown.

In one of my letters I said that a special chapter might be given upon dining in America. I do not think this is necessary, but I may say that a stranger at first finds a difficulty in getting enough to eat, until he is familiar with the bills of fare and the way dishes are prepared. I was frequently asked by an American friend during the first few days after landing, as a joke, whether I was wanting my dinner. To which I seriously answered yes, several times a day. As in many other matters in the cities, the American cuisine is after French models. A mutton chop such as we know it at home is never seen; soles are unknown. As was said in the *Saturday Review* the other day, however, " there is much in American cookery that English housekeepers would do well to borrow." The variety of dishes is astonishing. I have before me a bill of fare of the day, Thursday, 23rd September last, at one of the large sea-side hotels. There are oysters, lobsters, clams, soft-shell crabs, and little necks, all served in a variety of ways. Six soups to select from follow. Then come twelve kinds of fish, followed by entrees, by roast and boiled flesh and fowl, and by game. Twenty-five items swell the list of vegetables, in which our cousins excel. Potatoes, cooked in half a dozen ways, tomatoes, green corn, onions, rice, beans, mushrooms, macaroni, and succotash, besides a string of salads, relishes, and preserved fruits, with twenty-six kinds of pastry and ice creams !

But these are trifles. The great fact,—which was ever present to my mind, and which was brought home to me in a thousand ways, from the morning I stepped upon the quay by the Hudson River and was accosted by a Custom-house officer, to the day I embarked in the *Bothnia* on my return home,—was the American people. There, separated from us only by the ocean, are fifty millions of people, speaking our language, working hard late and early, prospering and happy, self-governed and strong. Unconsoled by the presence of a State Church, and yet possessing more places of worship per head of population than elsewhere; unprotected by a great costly standing army or navy, and yet secure; and even destitute of an aristocracy with hereditary privileges and power, yet unconscious of their poverty.

To travel in the United States is to witness the full meaning of the civilisation of the nineteenth century, untrammelled by prejudice or precedent. Do not let this be misconstrued as speaking in a strain derogatory of my own country. It is not so intended, for I am sufficiently antiquated, and unequal to the task of divesting myself of what may be called prejudice, to still believe that the best outcome of civilisation is yet to be found among English gentlefolk, where culture has gone hand in hand with breed. And I have an instinctive repugnance to nickel and veneer of all kinds.

Lord Beaconsfield in his most tawdry, recently published work, "Endymion," has gone out of his way to use a double-shotted sneer, when he makes one of his characters suggest the supposition that society in America is very like society in Manchester. And yet these American people, like the working and middle classes of England, have done great things, notwithstanding much opposition from the patrician class. It is not wise to sneer either at Manchester or America. Manchester has done the State some service, and they know it. The existence of the United States is an influence continuously operating on the Old World, which as time rolls on will gather force and become irresistible in changing much of the political and social structures that now look lasting. To my mind one of the sublimest episodes in the history of nations was seen after the suppression of the Southern Slaveholders' Revolt against the United States, when a vast and excited army, flushed with victory, was rapidly disbanded, and its soldiers returned to their peaceful avocations as citizens. Nor was the example of the United States Government less striking for its magnanimity when they forgave and set free the leading rebels, who had caused the expenditure of an unparalleled amount of blood and treasure. To their honour also be it remembered that they were willing to submit important claims to arbitration with respect to the pirate ship *Alabama*, built and launched in one of our chief ports, and which thence sailed forth on the high seas to burn and destroy the property of a friendly nation. These were two examples which will not be without effect in future history.

There is one matter of policy pursued by the United States which is distasteful to Englishmen especially, and that is their high protective tariff. And on this question I had frequent opportunities for discussion. We need not wonder, however, at the slow progress the doctrine of free exchange makes in the States, when we remember that even aided by a famine in Ireland how difficult a fight we had to establish the principle in our own country. Moreover our fight here was for the prime want of life, bread. There, food is produced in abundance, not only for themselves, but for all the world. And it is a protection of manufactures, not of bread-stuffs. But I have no doubt whatever that the common sense of America will settle this question, for light penetrates, and the principle of free exchange of commodities is as true and beneficent in its action as all other laws of the universe. And as only fifteen millions of people are directly interested, or believe that they are, in opposing this law, whilst the remaining thirty-five millions are sufferers to a large extent by the opposition, it is clearly a matter of light and knowledge, which Time will bring.

The extraordinary extent of inland navigation in the United States is without doubt one of the most commanding features of the country, which had, to a large extent, before the discovery of railway making, guided the spread of population and determined the sites of many cities. I think that few among us realise the fact, that there are four rivers on the continent of North America, any one of which is larger than all the rivers of the United Kingdom put together. There are more than sixty thousand miles of river, and over one hundred and fifty thousand square miles of lake, on the northern continent of America. The Lakes alone occupy an area equal to the whole extent of Great Britain and Ireland, with the Channel Islands and another Ireland added. These rough and ready comparisons will help us to estimate the attribute of vastness, which so characterises America. For two thousand miles almost, from the Atlantic seaboard inland, the land, rarely rising to mountain heights, is drained by the great arterial rivers, Missouri and Mississippi, with their many tributaries; some of these, take the Arkansas, the Tennessee, and the Ohio, being mighty streams that thread their way thousands of miles through rock and forest and mountain land. And yet at the beginning of this century, and even later, the population of the United States hung about the Atlantic sea-board, and may be said roughly not to have penetrated more than two or three hundred miles inland, except at New Orleans and along the banks of the great rivers, and stretching like a fringe around the Gulf of Mexico.

It was the discovery of gold in California that, acting like a loadstone upon the adventurous spirits both of the Old World and the New, drew the stream of population westward; and, although the excitement incidental to all auriferous discoveries has subsided, other not less valuable finds have attracted men thither from far and near. For on their way west, and especially on the vast western plains, virgin soil was found, prolific and inviting, with a climate so exhilarating and dry that wheat of the finest quality is grown, cut down, and threshed on the field, no housing necessary, in quantities sufficient to freight the navies of the world. Nature there, too, is prodigal of delicious fruits; and in the sublime solitudes of those far western valleys and along the slopes of the snow-crowned Sierras, it was reserved for our generation to discover forest trees, stupendous beyond the imagination of civilized man. These ideas of vastness and grandeur operate on the minds of men, and are an unseen influence ever at work. The people of the United States are the most instructed people in the world, and among the most law-abiding. The schoolhouse of New England was not planted in vain, and I hope it will be jealously guarded from priestly interference to all future time. There was sown the little seed which germinated and grew into the tree of liberty, and the defence of which has lifted the United States to a foremost place in the nations of the earth.

They are a nation of workers. Time will bring leisure when Art will grow upon American soil. There is even now no English poet who is more read and whose combination of mind and feeling has a deeper hold on the affections of the multitude than Longfellow; and for his cheery, delightful companionship who can compare with Oliver Wendel Holmes?

The American character has some blemishes which Time may change. Like the newly-made rich in the old world, there is too frequently a self-assertive tone which is not pleasant, and a want of deference which is painful to witness. But these are perhaps the exuberance of strength, and as time goes on an increased leisure may bring greater tranquillity of life and a repose of mind fruitful of good results.

Already I see the beginning of the new age ;—that activity in intellectual work which continually applies itself to practical affairs, and which has given us the sewing machine, the steam plough, the improved printing press, and a perfect host of inventions for economising human labour, will never pass away, but may in other generations work out its subtle life in creative art.

> "Let knowledge grow from more to more,
> But more of reverence in us dwell ;
> That mind and soul, according well,
> May make one music as before,
> But vaster."

I have in my short visit to the States seen a few of their chief cities, and, along with several places historically interesting, looked upon the grandest object there, Niagara. But I feel how little I have seen, and how much there is, especially for Englishmen, both to be seen in the United States, and to be studied in the development of the people and their institutions. It is the great country of the future, and I urge most strenuously all those who happen to read these lines to lose no chances of making themselves acquainted with the condition of men over the water, and better than all to go and see for themselves. With true insight our Laureate has sung :—

> "For I doubt not through the ages one increasing purpose runs
> And the thoughts of men are widened by the process of the suns."

In my travels in the States I was often reminded, without knowing why, of what had clung to my imagination, from the days when as an obscure worker in sympathy with the cause of justice and freedom, I read the words of our great countryman, in December, 1862, who, speaking at Birmingham of what was in his mind's eye, said :—" It may be but a vision, but I will cherish it. I see one vast confederation stretching from the frozen North in unbroken line to the glowing South, and from the wild billows of the Atlantic westward to the calmer waters of the Pacific main ;—and I see one people, and one language, and one law, and one faith, and over all that wide continent, the home of freedom, and a refuge for the oppressed of every race and of every clime."

THE

PASSION PLAY

AT

OBER-AMMERGAU, BAVARIA.

———

17th SEPTEMBER, 1871.

THE PASSION PLAY.

IN visiting Ammergau we did not go, as most travellers do, from Munich, but took a carriage at Innsbruck and drove leisurely, during two fine days, through most magnificent mountain scenery. The first couple of hours of our journey is along the valley of the Inn, on each side of which rise lofty mountains, rugged and barren along their highest ridges, but clothed with pines on the lower slopes. In the valley are broad, green meadows, through which the cold, rapid, and clear river flows. We ascend the mountains and reach a high plateau, on which is the village of Seefeld (higher than Snowdon), and on all sides tower the giants of the Bavarian Alps. A few hours' drive brings us through Mittenwald to Partenkirchen, gloriously placed in the centre of a ring of mountain peaks. And with this grand panorama to look back upon, we reach the charming Ammerthal; passing through the picturesque village of Ettal, we come in sight of a huge cross raised upon a high mountain cliff, which overhangs and points out Ammergau.

The village lies along a flat valley, straggling probably a distance of half a mile. The houses are well built, clean, and commodious. It is not an ordinary village. As we come near, we pass pedestrians of both sexes, and overtake vehicles with visitors, like ourselves, going to the Passion Play. We drive to the house of Madame Veit, to whom we had written for rooms and tickets, and are quickly billeted upon a tidy housewife in one of the many pleasant and clean cottages. There is a bit of garden, in which we may sit under the fruit trees and take tea. We look into the town; it is crowded with people eager to get something to eat and drink. All is bustle and noise there. In the crowd of men sitting round the numerous tables is one evidently the centre of a little circle. He has long hair and is enjoying his beer—it is Judas Iscariot. We live at the house of Jacobus the younger. I have asked many groups of children whether they act in the Passion Play; the answer is always that they do. All the children of the village take part in the performance. There are many priests here. No doubt they feel interested in keeping up the enthusiasm created by these representations.

There can be no doubt as to the religious character of this performance in the minds of the people. At the early hour of three in the morning the church bells began to toll out their invitations to come to mass. I looked out and saw various groups of peasants making their way there. At half-past five our little party went to the church—it was crowded, almost entirely with peasants, both men and women. There were very few visitors present. At the five altars priests were officiating, and in various parts of the service the congregation responded, men and women alternately, most heartily. There was much devotion. The music was very moving—the soprano and bass voices unusually fine. I have seldom witnessed a more impressive scene than this early mass in this remote village in Bavaria. And this special musical service was in preparation for the solemn representation of the Passion of the Lord and Saviour, whom these people worship, and the image of whose crucified body is placed before their eyes almost at every turn and winding of their highways and villages.

The early morning September mist had scarcely passed out of the valley and revealed the mountain sides, as the people crowded into the theatre, open for the most part to the sky. It is a singular sensation to sit in this theatre, so unlike all others of this age—and whilst waiting for the beginning of the drama, to look out upon the blue sky, the green meadows, the distant villages, and the pine covered hills, which form a sort of amphitheatre around us. On each side is a row of poplar trees; between them and the drop scene are the two openings which fairly represent streets in Jerusalem, and, again, are two balconies, representing the houses of Pilate and Annas. In and before these balconies certain important scenes are enacted.

Precisely at eight o'clock a gun is fired, the vast audience settle themselves down and are rapidly hushed to silence, the music gradually rises like a delicate odour, and the chorus enters. The chorus is composed of nineteen persons,—twelve women and seven men. These arrange themselves in a semicircle upon the stage and announce and describe the various scenes and tableaux, the leader of the chorus, John Dimmer, taking his place in the centre. He gives what may be called the recitative. They are picturesquely dressed in flowing robes, and they group themselves most artistically. The entrance of the chorus is most impressive by their dignified and graceful movements. The curtain rises, and the first tableau is before us. It is a representation of Adam and Eve driven out of Paradise by the Archangel with a flaming sword. The grouping is very picturesque, and it is wonderful that the *pose* can be maintained so long. This first tableau remained before us about three minutes. During this period the choir sing their explanation of the picture and its relation to the scene which is to follow. The second tableau represents the Adoration of the Cross. These two pictures symbolise the idea of the the play,—the fall and hope of man,—and precede the first scene of the drama, which is Christ's entry into Jerusalem. This is very beautifully worked out; many children, women, and men, with palm branches in their hands, precede and accompany Christ, who is seated upon an ass. These spread their garments before him. The whole play very faithfully adheres to the Scripture narrative both in action and text. Nothing can be more impressive than the calm, dignified manner of the Christ, as he, after dismounting, comes slowly before his followers toward the front of the stage, where the chief discourse is held. Although Mair and Lechner,—the Christ and the Judas of the play,— are wonderful actors, it is only right to say that all the acting by the men is fine. The Caiaphas is quite equal to the two named. The most trifling part is not left in careless hands. The women only play weakly, but their beauty, and the tenderness of their tones of voice, are some compensation for their inefficient acting. The face of the Virgin is a poem, and her voice is full of heart-breaking tenderness, but she and the other Marys are almost dull and frigid, when one would look for the intense anguish they are suffering to manifest itself in outward demonstration. At the vacant tomb of the risen Lord they are impassive—only at the sight of her son bearing the heavy cross does Mary put her feelings in her speech. And at this point in the play, there was a widely-spread response in the breasts of the audience. It may be the simple and wondrous story with which we are all so familiar from our earliest childhood, or the rare spectacle of a village population, for generations devoting themselves in their leisure to the study of dramatic art, impelled by a deep religious motive ; but without analyzing why,—there is certainly something extraordinary in the fact of three thousand people, and of these a large proportion of impatient English and Americans, sitting attentively with only one pause, to witness a performance which lasts from eight to nine hours.

During the movements of the crowd in the entry into Jerusalem, and in a manner which one does not notice until it is done, the scene is changed to the outer courts of the temple, with the money changers in full swing, and those who sell doves. Mair's acting here is fine ; his rebukes sting the Pharisees ; he overthrows the tables, and, taking cords, drives out with stripes the dealers from the courts of the Temple. Here the crowd supports him, but an adverse faction is created of the dealers and the Pharisees, which the chief priests observe and foment. Christ takes leave of his followers and with his disciples retires to Bethany.

The next scene in the drama is that of the Jewish Sanhedrim, in which Annas and Caiaphas figure prominently. The members of the high council hold an excited meeting on the recent doings of Christ, and the strongest feelings of exasperation are expressed against him. It is thought that one of the followers of Christ is susceptible to a bribe. A loudly expressed desire for retaliation upon Christ by the Pharisees and dealers follows—they are commissioned to find him out—and the meeting closes with dire resolutions and invoking the fathers of Israel.

The third scene, or act as it called, is Christ at Bethany. It is divided into three parts ; the walk with his disciples to the house of Simon, their talk by the way about his departure, then the meal taken together in the house where Martha waits upon the Lord and his disciples, and where Mary Magdalene comes and casts herself before the Master. She anoints his head and feet with costly ointment. The grouping here was picturesque, but the acting of the Magdalene very formal. The parting of Christ (which follows) and his mother was very beautifully rendered—it was a quiet, simple, tender leave-taking, full of deep, unspoken grief on the part of Mary, as she embraces her steadfast son, upon whom to look is to feel strong. He gently leaves his mother with her women and Lazarus, and the disciples follow him. This was a brief and beautiful scene; and there was a decided sadness upon the audience during its representation.

The fourth scene gives the journey to Jerusalem; here the temptation of Judas occurs. He lingers behind the rest of the disciples, and whilst soliloquising about the value of the lost valuable ointment is overtaken by one and then others of the dealers, who offer him money to betray the Master into their hands. After much agitation he succumbs to their repeated pressure, and promises to accept their reward.

The fifth act is one of the most impressive scenes in the whole play, and yet it is the least assisted by external theatrical aids. It is the scene of the last supper—Christ and the twelve apostles are seated around the table, grouped as in Leonardo da Vinci's picture—he speaks to them in the words we read in the Gospels. The Scripture narrative is acted and spoken. The Lord washes the disciples' feet—it is very impressive in its simplicity. Then after the washing of feet he breaks bread and gives the disciples, each one, to eat—followed by his taking round the cup and saying, "This is my blood, drink ye all of it. Do this in remembrance of me." Then comes the question of who is the one to betray the Lord. Jesus places a sop in the mouth of Judas, who starts as possessed of a devil, and as Christ utters the words, "What thou doest do quickly," he rushes out as with an irresistible impulse. Afterwards comes the talk with Peter, and the words "Thou, Peter, wilt deny me." The Christ of this scene is a masterpiece of delicate acting. It is subdued and tranquil, yet with a sense of godlike calm power that nothing can disturb.

The sixth scene shows us once more the Jewish Sanhedrim. The meeting of the council is very excited, and all except two of its members are loud and vehement in desiring revenge against Jesus.

Joseph of Arimathea and Nicodemus speak in his favour, and are declared by Caiaphas to be unworthy to sit in the assembly. They retort, and there is much discussion, high and strong. The scene is splendidly acted. Judas is brought in, and, after some bargaining, the money he is to have is counted out to him. With the feeling of a miser, he grasps each coin, and the details of his arrangement are discussed and settled. The assembly is excited with wrathful satisfaction at the prospect of seizing the person of Christ. Nicodemus and Joseph leave the hall—they will not be party to the contract with Judas. The scene ends excitedly with cries of "Death to him—let him die."

At this stage of the drama there is a pause of about an hour. And here I ought to say that before each of the scenes proper to the play there are two or more tableaux, the subjects taken from the Scriptures, and having some reference, real or symbolical, to that which is to follow. These tableaux are accompanied by songs and choruses, explanatory, which are sung either by one voice or the whole chorus, or in alternate strophes by either half of the singing chorus. The music is always pleasing; sometimes it is deeply impressive, penetrating the depths of one's emotional nature. It is in these tableaux the children mostly take their little parts, and are well seen in the living picture of the fall of manna in the wilderness; also in the two tableaux of the brazen serpent lifted up by Moses. In these beautiful representations there are two or three hundred persons—men, women, and children, some very young.

The second division of the play is introduced with the tableau of Adam condemned to earn his bread by the sweat of his brow. This is a very effective picture. Adam and Eve, in sheepskins, and seven children are grouped in various attitudes of work and play. They are living statues. The seventh act of the drama is the garden of Gethsemane, and the events and words of the Scripture narrative are faithfully adhered to in the representation. It is painfully realistic; the interest is intense when, during the agony of Christ, as he prays for the third time, an angel appears, ministering to him. Then come the soldiers, the crowd, and the betrayer—the incident of Peter smiting the servant of the high priest and Christ healing the wound—the falling down of the soldiers upon Christ's saying, "I am he;" then his being led away, ill-used by the soldiers and the crowd. We next see Christ led before Annas, the high priest—who awaits his arrival with impatience upon the balcony of his house overlooking one of the streets of Jerusalem. The priests have now gained the crowd of people to their views; after a painful scene of questioning by Annas, he sends Jesus to Caiaphas. The crowd press around him, jeering; the soldiers insult him and push him before them. Jesus is led before Caiaphas and his subordinates, and the false witnesses are brought forth. It is decided to send him to the hall of judgment. Then follows the scene in the porch, where Jesus is rudely and violently treated by the soldiers. Also, the scene where Peter denies Christ. This is most dramatically worked out; it is painted with the minutest fidelity to the text of the gospel, and every actor in the play seems to feel the reality of his part.

The tenth scene represents the Sanhedrim once more, which declares that Christ must die. Judas, after wandering about restlessly, comes and wishes to undo what he has done. After much altercation and violent recrimination, he throws down the money which he had received and rushes away. Then we see him alone, suffering from intense remorse at the ruin he has made; his agony becomes fearful, and in his despair he hangs himself. The tableau which precedes the despair of Judas is one of great power. It is Cain a wanderer and a vagabond upon the face of the earth.

The eleventh act represents Christ brought before Pilate. This and the two subsequent appearances of Christ before Pilate are perhaps the most powerful scenes in the play. The last scene before Pilate's house is exceedingly exciting and lifelike, and during its movement there are shown some of the most artistically arranged groups of men and women I have ever beheld on any stage.

The twelfth act shows us Christ before Herod, to whom Pilate has referred the case, as being in his special jurisdiction. In the thirteenth act Pilate has given up Jesus to be scourged, and in this scene all the brutal mockery of the soldiery was delineated. The fourteenth act shows the triumph of the priestly element, which, working upon the populace, had brought an overwhelming clamour to Pilate for the death of Jesus, and after a long and wonderfully sustained scene, in which Jesus maintains a sublime indifference to taunts and insults, and in which Pilate does much to try to save Christ from the ferocious Jews, he at length breaks the stick and hands him over to be crucified. Two thieves are also brought out, and are taken away with the Christ. The triumph of the priests is complete, the crowd is wild with savage delight.

The fifteenth act is appropriately introduced by three tableaux: First, Isaac carrying wood to the altar upon which he is to be laid; second, Moses raising the brazen serpent; third, the children of Israel looking up to the brazen serpent raised by Moses in the wilderness. These are all living pictures, and they are accompanied by soul-subduing music—the refrain,—

> "Betet an und habet dank,
> Der den kelch der leiden trank,
> Geht nun in den Kreuzestod
> Und versöhnt die welt mit Gott!"*

following twice after each musical exposition. Then the chorus withdraws, and we see Mary the virgin mother, Magdalene, and other women, with John, approaching down one of the streets of Jerusalem. They pause sadly, as they with us, hear loud shouts proceeding from an excited multitude who are coming through the streets at the other side of the great stage. These harsh shouts are from the crowd which moves along with Christ, who is now seen bearing the massive cross, under which he walks with difficulty. He is guarded by Roman soldiers and attended by four executioners. At length he sinks beneath the heavy load, and Simon of Cyrene, who happens to be walking near, is seized by the Roman guard and made to carry the cross in place of Christ. Meanwhile the sorrowing mother weeps and her women raise their lamentations as the mournful procession draws nearer. Then comes Veronica. All the women are weeping. But Jesus pauses and speaks to them, saying in a tender voice. "Weep not for me,

---

* "Worship and give thanks!
Who the cup of suffering drank,
Goes now on the cross to die
And atones the world with God!"

O daughters of Jerusalem, but for yourselves and for your children;" and then the slow, sad march goes on. This is the most moving scene in the play—the impassioned, loving tones of Mary as she speaks out of her deep anguish to her suffering son, penetrate every heart. Very shortly follows the culminating incident of this absorbing drama. The scene opens and we see three crosses, not yet lifted up, but with the two thieves already fastened, and Jesus being nailed upon the cross. Presently they are raised, placed in the ground, and made secure.

The inscription, "This is Jesus, the King of the Jews," is placed by order of Pilate over the head of Christ. The crowd and soldiers jeer and scoff. The thieves each speak to Christ,—one derisively and the other with penitence,—and Jesus replies. After a while Jesus faintly speaks; one of the soldiers then gives him vinegar on a sponge. He sinks his head, and cries, "Eli, Eli, Lama Sabachthani,"—his head now falls forward—he is dying—the thunder peals—there is darkness; the bystanders, the soldiers, the executioners, even the high priests, are troubled. The executioners ascend the ladders to break the two thieves, and one shudders to see them die beneath the heavy strokes. The body of Christ does not undergo this ignominy. But the captain of the guard thrusts a spear into his side, and one starts as the blood rushes from the wound. Soon Joseph of Arimathea comes to claim the body armed with an order from Pilate. Then follows the taking down from the cross—the body is tenderly released from the cross, and carefully lowered by the friends and followers of the dead Lord. At the foot of the cross are the three Marys, and other women, with John, the disciple whom Jesus loved. The body is placed upon a linen sheet, the head of the dead Christ resting upon his mother's knees. It is a very mournful sight. Then the body is enveloped in white linen and carried by Joseph and Nicodemus to the sepulchre, against the entrance to which is placed a great stone.

When the curtain rises for the seventeenth scene the grave is guarded by four Roman soldiers, who speak to each other about the late crucifixion. Suddenly there is thunder and an earthquake, which throws down the stone from the door of the tomb, and Christ, radiant and majestic, walks forth. This would be a fitting end to the play; the interest to this point is unceasing and unbroken; but what follows is the women and disciples at the tomb—then the Pharisees, who wish to bribe the soldiery. Then Christ appears to Mary Magdelene in the garden.

The eighteenth and last act is a tableau representing the ascension of the glorified Christ, the chorus singing joyously as he ascends. And as the long shadows of the poplar trees stretch across the place, and the sun sinks below the western hills, the curtain falls and the Ammergau Passion Play is over. Whether we look at the large number of persons engaged in the play, the great care bestowed upon every detail, the high character of the delineation, the vast audience gathered from all countries, the remote and picturesque situation in a quiet Bavarian mountain village, the character of the actors, the motives which impel them to their work, the marvellous finish and effect of their effort—it is without doubt one of the most extraordinary exhibitions of our times, and one which makes a profound impression upon those who see it, quite apart from their creed or their want of one.

The play is over, and the crowds of people who have sat so long with intense attention to this mournful drama, are rapidly disappearing. By seven o'clock the village is nearly deserted, and by nine the lights are almost out. Throughout the three days we have been here we have seen nothing like the faintest approach to disorder, notwithstanding the great crowd and the profusion of good beer, except in the case of two fat priests, who, late one night, passed us on our way home, reeling drunk.

THREE WEEKS

IN

NORWAY;

A SERIES OF LETTERS

Written in JUNE, 1860.

LIST OF OUTLINES.

BERGEN .	to face page 84
NAERODAL . .	101
NAERODAL	102
STALHEIM FOSS	103
NEAR GUDVANGEN	103
STŸVE ON NAERO FJORD .	104
NAERO FJORD	105
NAERO FJORD . .	105
NEAR HUSUM	110
NEAR HUSUM	111
NEAR BORGUND	111
BORGUND CHURCH	112

Geo Crozier.   STALHEIM FOSS.   Tho. Letherbrow.

THREE WEEKS IN NORWAY.

SAILED from Hull, in the *Anna*, on the morning of Saturday, 2nd June, 1860, dropping down the turbid Humber to the sea about five o'clock. Bright, clear morning, but very cold; and as we put off the pilot at the Spurn, the wind freshened, the sun became less bright, and a grey haze overspread the sky, sending me down to a breakfast I was not destined to consume, for the inevitable sea serpent had already got me in his tortuous folds, and the green sickness of a landsman overspread my vision as I took a place at that otherwise cheerful board.   .

On Sunday night, as I walked on to the deck of the vessel, the moon, large and beautiful, sailed as it were out of the sea into the silent night; turning from her full-orbed gaze, I looked upon the outlines of a dark low line of rocks, with higher elevations in a second line beyond, snow-capped; over these dark masses of cloud lay sullenly in long deep lines, in striking contrast with the broad band of orange-tinted sky that marked the lingering light of the setting sun. It was my first sight of Gamlé Norge (Old Norway). The water was now calm, only the ripple of the ship's advance disturbed the silence, but the air was extremely cold, and again I sought my snug berth. As I lie awake, there is a cessation in the throbbings of that great heart whose pulsations had so regularly propelled us; and, in expectancy, I hear a few Norsk words. We are taking on board a Norwegian pilot, who has put off from the coast, though distant some miles. The first is always taken, and if one comes out he must be taken. At 2-45 the sun rose over the huge dark rocks, and about seven o'clock we near the narrow entrance of the fjord leading to our port, and we all meet on deck once more with pleasant faces. There are only five passengers from Hull, and one is a Norwegian.

It is a sail of about twenty-six English miles from the entrance of the rocks, and inside the water is smooth as a lake, with rocks, dark and barren, rising most picturesquely on each side. As we steam up this lake, here and there are sweet patches of rich green; a small house, with boat moored to an adjacent rock; perhaps a few cottages and a small church; occasionally on some high projection a cow or two crop what little provender they can from the almost, to us, bare-looking rock upon which they stand; villa-like residences appear in sheltered nooks, and most attractive they are, suggesting the refinements of life and cheerful family circles on the winter nights.

The rocks are gneiss mainly, old as the foundations of the planet, grim and gaunt. Grander views open before us as we advance inland; still the same succession of green patches and pretty villas; frequently fishing boats, light and buoyant, pass us rapidly. We make a rather sharp turn, and, with somewhat of surprise, come upon Bergen. We are at the head of the fjord; Bergen is at the base of that huge, almost bare rock, that rises from the sea a thousand feet. An English yacht lies at anchor in the bay; and close in shore are numerous fishing smacks, their high prows rising considerably, like those of the vikings of old, above the half-open deck of the vessels. The same style of boat in which, a thousand years ago, the Northmen shoaled upon our coasts, and swarmed over our rich and accessible flats. The town stretches round the head of this water, which runs up between like the thin end of a pear; the red-tiled roofs straggling in tiers or terraces up the hill side from the water's extreme edge.

The sky is clear, and of a soft blue; it is a lovely June morning. After a very trifling formality, we are passed through the custom-house; no passports asked for. We loiter up the hill, gazing at the strange costumes and the pretty faces, for already we have seen several Scandinavian beauties, and we stop at the house of Madame Sontum, where Brown, Jones, Robinson, and Smith, the four English passengers just arrived, soon form a group of equal attraction for an admiring and good humoured crowd.

BERGEN.

The peculiar beauty of Bergen, its quaint wooden houses, every window ornamented with flowers, is very manifest as we walk to make our respects to the British vice-consul. In this latitude, that, I think, of Petersburg and the Shetland Islands, we find in profusion, in the windows, roses, fuchsias, and lilies in the better class of houses, and I do not remember any house without its flowers.

The streets are clean, and a crowd of life is moving about the town. The ordinary English costume is the respectable inhabitant, engaged in mercantile affairs, but that is the exception ; there are many strange and very curious dresses that stand out by the brightness of their colours from this varied crowd. The female peasants from Hardanger have dark-blue, close-fitting bodices and kirtles, with a white and red richly-embroidered breastwork, close-fitting blue and red caps, and braided hair ; whilst here and there may be seen peasants from the more distant interior, with a profusion of gold and silver ornaments upon their bosoms. It is a great fair, and sunny June, and we see Bergen under a favourable aspect as regards light, colour, and gaiety. In the shops we notice many articles of protection from rain—oil-skin coats, hats, boots, &c., and immense wooden shoes : it is the wettest town in Norway.

There is a considerable crowd, but nothing remotely approaching to excitement ; the lives of these people flow more tranquilly than those of our good folks at home. There are soldiers, though, even here, for even this craggy coast of Norway, facing the rude Atlantic, has attractions for one of "the Great Powers," who has no claims there. We watched their drill ; the artillery, a very fair, soldierly-looking set of men, who could fight like the ancient sea-kings upon occasion.

As we pass by the burial-grounds, I notice over the grass-grown graves are placed wooden crosses, carved and gilt ; some of them twined with wreaths of everlastings, and many of the tombs covered with flowers.

On the German side of the town is the Bourse, where to-day many merchants do congregate, and along the quay a slight attempt at bustle prevails. A deep and unmistakeable odour of cod liver oil and much fish, saturates the air in this neighbourhood.

We visit a small picture gallery and are shown a series of drawings, exhibiting various stages of leprosy, which extends frightfully throughout Norway, chiefly on the western coast, and more north than south. There are here two large hospitals for those afflicted with this terrible evil.

We return to Madame Sontum's to dine. Fish is served; again fish, fish curiously disguised, and again fish. It is overdoing a good thing. You take, as a relief, some pudding. Vain delusion; it is again fish, in another of his multitudinous transmutations. Beer, moderately good, and fair claret, with a cup of coffee and *petit verre*, *à la Française*.

In the early evening we had a delightful drive round the suburbs of Bergen, through the kindness of a Norwegian friend, to whom I had letters of introduction, and whose fine spirit of hospitality and goodwill can never be forgotten. We returned through pleasant long avenues of lime and birch, down by the water side, where the burghers spend their summer evenings, and the young couples while away their sweetest hours. We return home a little before ten o'clock, quite daylight, a rich warm glow filling the western sky. At eleven o'clock, still light enough in the streets to read with perfect ease a letter I am about to post.

The good citizens are abed; the streets are deserted and quiet; we walk along with our friend towards his home at the other end of the town. As we near the ancient gateway we hear a loud, unearthly noise—or as of some maudlin drunkard, who roareth in the mad dream of his cups as he hiccoughs reeling home. There is no one near. The sound comes, as it were, out of the air, and is most marvellous. "The night is clear, the wind is still—it is half-past eleven," in deep tones, is moaned through a huge speaking trumpet by the watchman from the Kirke Tower, and we feel that we have gone back centuries. Nothing was more quaintly impressive than this finish to our day in Bergen, though its first aspect had appealed to us somewhat ludicrously.

The people of Bergen are practical followers of Franklin, in the matter of "early to bed and early to rise;" as we passed through the town the shops were gradually opening, although barely six o'clock. In the early morning, the scenes, the same we had driven over last evening, wore a new aspect, and we felt that we were having more than usual good fortune in the weather.

The road to Garnæs begins with fine sweeping undulations, each eminence commanding views of Bergen, the bay, and distant fjord. The last of these views, of the lofty mountains, the calm shining fjord, the little fleet of fishing boats in the harbour, the long line of town, straggling up the hill, and thinly veiled in morning mist, the dome Kirche in the centre, with the sweetly luxuriant foreground, lying in shadow of the mountain, made a picture never to be forgotten.

Buckling the burdens upon our backs in earnest, we passed away from Bergen. As we walked along we were strongly reminded of Borrowdale, in Cumberland; crags and richly-wooded hills, with a small tranquil lake sleeping in their midst, about a Norsk, or seven English miles, from Bergen. Then come a series of rocks and country, suggesting Bettws-y-Coed, in North Wales, but more of it, and continuous. Then a long stretch of wild uncultivated rugged moorland, a clear mountain stream rushing down the valley, and wild mountain sides sloping gently from either side. We had now walked about eight or nine miles; it was very hot, and the knapsacks were so far disagreeable companions. We had noticed several small carts on the road containing produce, and as another was approaching we took the opportunity for our first essay in Norsk. "Have you any milk?" Puzzled look of peasant in reply. "Milk?" A gleam of intelligence. "Ya!" "Can we have some?" The difficulty now was how to measure or get at it. "What for that tub?" said I, pointing to a small keg that stood prominently inviting in the cart. "Seven skillings," said the man. "Let me have it, here are eight;" and, knocking off the top, we drank long and deep at our purchase, largely refreshed by the rich unctious liquid, and pleased, of course, at the success of our early endeavour to make ourselves understood by words. The heartiness with which the farmer shook hands when he gave us "tak," or thanks, as is the custom, evidenced that he considered eight skillings as an excellent equivalent for the two quarts of milk.

A further walk of seven or eight miles over varied country brought us to Garnæs, on the south-western shore of the Oster Fjord, a noble expanse of water, stretching right and left many miles. Hence we took boat for Dalevaagen (about midway up the fjord), a distance of 17 or 18 miles. The scenery along this fjord is grand; the hills are not more than 1,000 feet, but they are thickly wooded to the water's edge, and, when not clothed with forest, of broken and picturesque outline. In one reach of this great lake is a beautiful waterfall, falling at a great elevation in one huge mass, then quickly spreading, fan-like, over the scattered rocks below. Our enjoyment heightened with every turn of the boat, and the magnificent pass into which the fjord narrows at Dalevaagen seemed to culminate the excitement. We walked through the solitary pass, darkened into gloom, almost, by the grandeur of its rocks and woods, passing a small village on the way where noisy revelry was rampant. One or two of the most hideous human faces grinned disagreeably upon us, drunk and madly gesticulating, as we went by.

From Dalevaagen to Dalseidet is about four miles and a half. At Dalseidet, we both exclaimed, was the finest single view we had seen during the day, a mighty expanse of calm water, with thickly wooded mountains, dipping almost perpendicularly to the lake. It is another arm of the Oster Fjord, over which we took boat to the next station.

In this hour's pull across the fjord from Dalseidet to Bolstadoren, the magical effect of the soft twilight and the perfect calm upon the water was marvellous. We rode in silence, and I found, in talking over our feelings afterwards, that my companion had experienced the same strange sensation of being, as it were, spell-bound with the witchery of the scene. Had the immense rock, towards which we were advancing without any prospect of an outlet, opened like a scene, I should not, I think, have been more surprised. The peculiar taciturnity and sad expression of face of the old boatman who sat nearest to us, added to the interest. It was altogether an ineffaceable scene, and I felt that we need no longer wonder that superstitious belief in elves and fairies held its ground. In one form or another may the heart's deep feeling out of which they grow, for ever live, weaving its fine fancies and high imaginings into robes of light.

Arrived at Balstadoren about ten o'clock, after a long day. Quite daylight. Excellent station; good comfortable supper, ham and eggs, best thing we have had since leaving England in the commissariat department; the management of which, upon the division of labour principle, is in the hands of my companion, a rare genius in the higher regions of gastronomic art.

The walk from Bolstadoren station—prettily placed between the hills—to the Evanger Vand is along a bank of the river connecting the two fjords. This river, swollen with the melting snows, rushed along the valley with great force. There is considerable cultivation here, and the road is as through a park grounds. The Evanger Vand is a beautiful lake, about four English miles long, surrounded by lofty hills, with farms dotted along their sides at frequent intervals. Here and there, as we pass near the shore, is a shelving rock, rich with a carpet of sweet violets that waft their perfume through the sunny air; now comes a patch of luxuriant grass and clover, whilst higher the abundant pine rises many-terraced, and the snow still in heavy patches crowns the scene.

Evanger is pleasantly situated at a corner of the lake; a few houses sufficiently scattered to form a group round the neat little white and red church, with a background of wooded hills, make the first sight of this village eminently picturesque. At Evanger we had a short delay, caused by the sudden illness of my friend. The people were very kind, and, after we were able to make ourselves understood, took much pains to assist us. Hired a carriole to next station, and were informed by the landlord at Evanger that in our way we should find a man who could speak English, whom the skyds-karl (car driver) should find for us, with a view to obtaining information about the next station. The country is very beautiful, more cultivated, with much wood, and loftier hills; the streams, still swollen with snow and rain, most musical. So far as the flora indicates, we might be in England. In the meadows, the marsh marigold and lady-smock of old Chaucer are profusely scattered. Violets, buttercups, and daisies abound. Among trees—pine, birch, and ash predominate. Butterflies, blue, yellow, and white, just as at home, flutter in the sunny air. It is perfect spring; nature is still robed in her freshest green; and the birds are singing their liveliest songs. We hear the cuckoo and the corn-crake loud and long; and flitting about constantly on heavier wing, common as our thrush, is the magpie.

As we enter the village of ——, the skyds-karl announces that T—— H—— is to be found here, and, pulling up, he asks a villager to find him. There is evidently some festivity in the village; we hear shouts, and one or two women in holiday dress peep out of doors. Whilst we wait, a tall and grave-looking old man, with much seriousness, almost amounting to solemnity, comes to speak with us; and he carries in his hands a large wooden bowl. It is filled to the brim with ale. "Skole, skole," he says, and drinks, handing the bowl to me. "Skole, skole," I reply, and drink deeply. I was in excellent condition to enjoy the proffered hospitality. By this time a small crowd had gathered round us, and each one had been asked where T—— H—— was, for that two Englishmans were here. We became rather anxious to go, after waiting some time, as we had no very urgent reason for taxing the missing gentleman's time, but it was clear that upon this occasion Englishmen were in too high repute to be allowed to go away quietly.

I was beckoned to follow one of the elders of the men, of whom some dozen had now assembled round our carriole, and I went along with him into one of the houses in the village; leading me to the foot of the stairs, like a grand chamberlain, he politely bowed me to ascend, and upon entering the upper room I found what was the cause of all the feast and merry-making. A bride and bridegroom sat to receive their friends; and, as an Englishman (of whom Mr. Williams has truly said the Norwegians have the highest respect, and consider them all lords or M.P.'s), I was thus solemnly asked to walk upstairs and drink the health of the happy couple. The room was decorated with the family chests, arranged on all sides, and the clothes of the bride and bridegroom spread around. No doubt there were many presents among the articles I saw. The bride was very prettily dressed, and certainly reminded me of our best ballet dancers, with longer petticoats and no crinoline. The ornaments upon the breast were numerous and sparkling, of gold and silver. The Norwegian women are very fond of trinkets, that is certain. The costume was a short petticoat, blue; red boddice, with white sleeves; with ornamented breastplate or stomacher of beadwork, on a dark ground; the long hair carefully braided. The bridegroom was dressed ordinarily, black vest and trousers, and in his shirt sleeves. I was again reminded of "Sonnambula" and the theatre; it was truly picturesque.

I was asked to sit down, and with considerable formality three glasses of beer were poured out, and rising, the bride, bridegroom, and myself, each took a glass, and, knocking them together, I wished them severally "skole." Then they drank my health. By this time one of the fathers-in-law came in, and I had to repeat the ceremony with him. After I had "skoled" about half-a-dozen times, a mother-in-law appeared with food—bread, cheese, and flesh—and a new knife of the bridegroom was offered to me, and I was requested to sit down at the table and eat. Of course, I complied with this hospitable request; and again, but this time with greater ceremony, out of a large silver cup, evidently a family relique, I was asked to "skole." This cup passed round; it contained a very disagreeable compound; I should think a sort of sacramental marriage wine of mixed bitters and sweets, that is only taken once in a lifetime.

Happily, I had with me a few small articles which I conceived would be useful to the wife and a trifling memento for the husband, which I ventured to offer; they were received with much gratification. We were once more "skoled," and now the bride and bridegroom offered to go out to the company assembled in the adjoining barn, prepared for the occasion, where fiddling and dancing were rife. The smiling couple were received with loud shouts; they wished me to join them in the dance. Possessing little skill in the sphere of the light fantastic toe, I had some doubts as to whether I should not bring disgrace on my nationality in this matter (for the Norwegians love dancing, and are critical), but as I was led to a buxom damsel near the bride, there was no escape, and the next moment found me in the sweet giddiness of a rapturous waltz. Good heavens! What an excitement! Round and round, in thrilling proximity. At length the fiddling ceases, and we offer our fair and blooming partners the great skole bowl, at which they drink. By this time T. H. had been found; and after receiving the information from him we desired, I asked him to translate a few phrases of thanks for myself and friend for the great favour they had so kindly given us. And as a final skole, in which I was joined by the whole strength of the company, I gave them

"Gamlé Norge." This was received with rapturous acclamation. In return, Mr. T. H. sang "God save the Queen," and we were dismissed with three times three, and one cheer more.

There was much in this village festival to please and admire in its unmistakeable gaiety and simplicity, and but for the unfortunate drinking that is always present, it would seem to be quite arcadian. In the country districts such as this, the wedding gatherings and festivities continue several days, sometimes a week, and considerable drunkenness, with other incidental evils, result.

About an English mile or so from the village we passed a very fine waterfall, and in a short time came in sight of the Voss Vand, a large lake; the small town of Vossevangen at its head. Many villages are scattered along the hills on either side, and large pine forests stretch around and upwards, losing themselves in masses of snow.

The peasantry here are a fine, hardy race; the dress of the women very picturesque. The invariable rule here is to salute as one passes with a cheerful " God dagen " or " God aften." It became evident that the wedding ale had somewhat inspired our skyds-karl, as the carriole rushed wildly over the undulating road. Without springs, though with long slender shafts, it is, at first, by no means an agreeable sensation to feel yourself going helter skelter down hill, with the knowledge that if your pony should stumble, you and the carriole will likely enough roll over a bank some hundreds of feet above the noisy stream you hear rushing along the dale.

By-and-by we reach Vossevangen, where we find a very comfortable station and obliging hostess. The church had been a very pleasant centre to our picture for several miles, and upon near approach showed most picturesquely against the dark pine-covered mountains beyond. It is said to have been built in the thirteenth century; very simple, of wood, with tower and graceful spire, and bell most musical. The houses cluster round the church, here as elsewhere, as if in those early days of its erection they had sought its protection, as well from the outward storms of nature as for the spiritual overshadowing of which it is significant.

There are no inns in Norway, except at the capital and in the largest towns; but at distances of from seven to ten miles English on all the great roads, there are houses, appointed by government and under periodical inspection, for the reception of travellers, and bound to furnish the means of locomotion either at call or upon a couple of hours' delay, according as the station, as it is called, is rated "fast" or "ordinary." On all the great post roads the traveller by carriole will meet with little delay ; in fact, the Storthing has decreed, we were informed, that on and after the 1st of July all stations shall be "fast." This will be a great advantage to all future travellers.

At the Vossevangen Station, or B. Jersins' hotel, as a recent sign denotes, I made my way into the kitchen and initiated the gude wife or "huusmoderen" in the mysteries of making a strong cup of tea, after the English fashion ; and I should strongly recommend all English travellers to take this commodity with them, and infuse it for themselves, unless they wish to experiment upon their stomachs. Having so far succeeded in the good graces of the hostess, the rest of our stay here was very cosy and most agreeable. We had excellent beef, well cooked ; wholesome potatoes, and, for the first time, good coffee. We were fortunate also in obtaining very fair Madeira here, at the very moderate cost of three marks four skillings, or 2s. 8d. a bottle. A Norwegian dollar is worth about 4s. 2d. English. Five marks, or 120 skillings, make a dollar.

In the evening, my companion, who was unwell, retired ; and I endeavoured to acquire a little knowledge of Norsk, under the kind tuition of a most agreeable and beautiful madame. It is surprising how rapidly one progresses in expression under the refining and exciting influences of bright eyes and a sweetly musical voice. I shall ever hold in most grateful memory the twilight hours upon the quaint verandah at Voss, with its charming broken English and monosyllabic Norsk.

Leaving our knapsacks at this temporary home, we started, on Thursday morning, on a detour from the main road of about fifty miles, for the Voring Voss, the "lion" of the South of Norway.

The road winds over undulating ground, and through sombre pine forests, for several hours. Ascending to higher elevations, we had extensive views of the far-stretching, rich, green valleys, with their swollen rushing rivers of clear water, musical with the roar of many mountain falls. It is yet too early in the year for the cattle to ascend the mountains; and the melodious tinkle of the kine bell floats through the fragrant air. About six miles from Graven, the road, ascending almost until now comes abruptly upon the head of a magnificent valley. The stream, of considerable volume, alongside of which we had a short way walked, leaping down 200 feet or more, then spreading out over broken crags in boiling surge, plunges under a bridge a little way down the vale. The road rapidly descends by zig-zags, then winds in sweet curves along the stream; rich knolls, with their solitary farms, are scattered along the dale in picturesque distance; and on each side tower mighty rocks, thinly spread with pines, and washed with falls from the snow-covered mountain heights beyond. Over the whole glorious scene streams bright sunlight and huge cloud.

As we walk we are overtaken by a returning wedding party, with the elders of whom we have what small converse our Norsk allows. Two carts carry the older women and children of the party, for the entire families had met at the nuptial gathering; the younger women plodding barefooted, occasionally taking a short turn in the carts by way of rest. Cheerful, contented, tranquil people, most anxious to give information and to reciprocate goodwill. Undisturbed by the political agitations which sweep over the great continent, they repose serenely in their happy valley, almost unconscious whether a Bourbon or a Bonaparte rides the imperial horse.

We walk down this luxuriant valley; for a while we sit by the clear rushing stream, listening to its music and the chorus of multitudinous falls and woods. It is a scene of surpassing beauty, and we feel its wondrous power in the emotions that surge over our hardened souls, like the river gushing over the rocks.

At Over-Vassenden we take boat across the lake to Graven, where, by an accident, we make the acquaintance of Captain ——, a Norwegian, who, in the finest spirit of hospitality, entertained us; stirring our nationality by speaking to us in English. We held quite a small revel here. Our native tongue, combined with real home-brewed malt liquor, were luxuries we had not hoped for, and their realisation raised us to jubilant heights of enjoyment. Our kind host led the way, and pointed us to the path over the fjeld—an exhilarating walk of about ten miles. The snow lay in thick patches across our path, at the highest elevation about four feet deep, delightfully cooling taken as an ice. As we descended from the wild moorland of the fjeld, upon Ulvik, the opening view was magnificent: lofty mountains in the near distance, with well-cultivated and thickly-wooded land in gentle slopes, descending like a fringe to the edge of a calm vast expanse of water, the head of a branch of the great Hardanger Fjord. The white church of Ulvik stands on a small promontory in the foreground, and many newly-painted white and red houses dot the green hills around. It is evening as we reach the shore, and the rich colouring of the sunlight falls on the hills. We call a boat, and shortly are gliding along the edge of the fjord. In a short time we have glimpses up the Ose Fjord, darkened by the shadow of the lofty mountains that divide it from the waters of Ulvik, and grander in its gloom. By-and-by we reach the Hardanger Fjord, wider considerably, than those we have seen, the mountains on each side and around rising to loftier heights. In the distance are deep lines of unbroken snow. Sunset, and its lingering glories, have gone; the sky is grey; with the overspreading cloud comes a wind that swells the water, so as to give straining work to our boatmen; but away they go, never flinching, and we make the south side, where there is the shelter of high rocks. Near midnight we came in sight of our haven, and by twelve o'clock are in the station at Vik. Not without a little noise, for the good people have quietly retired to bed; and during the first comfortable hour's sleep it is difficult to persuade anybody of the occasion for early rising.

At length we are admitted, and the whole half-dressed family, dog included, are tumultuously scuffling on our behalf and the boatmen's whom we have asked to sup. We obtain coffee—indifferent, bread—stale; and, after a brief rest, set off with a guide to the Foss. An hour's pull over the lake to Saebo is the first stage, then a long walk on the bank of the river that comes rushing wildly down, tearing and roaring over huge broken rocks. Talking is useless, except in the quieter reaches, so we stride along in single file, silently. It is quite daylight, in fact there is never darkness here at this season. We stay a short time watching the troubled stream and the varying hues of the morning sky. Then comes a long draught of rich milk at a small farm, with numerous cows, and quite a population of goats. Twice we cross the swollen, whirling stream by small wooden bridges, still we march on, always ascending, over a rude path made of large stones.

The valley is very grand : broken, irregular masses of rock, piled confusedly at intervals, over which we mount or wind slowly round ; lofty crags, often perpendicular, two and three thousand feet above our heads, their broken and jagged outlines clearly defined against the clear blue heavens. Impetuous cataracts rush over these heights and leap from ledge to ledge, or trail their vast lengths of beautiful spray.

A few scattered birches dot the rocks, and here and there on a level patch of green is a solitary farm.

After walking four or five miles up this valley, we leave the river to our left, and commence a gradual ascent up the face of the terminal rock of this deep gorge, which, at a short distance, seems to be a sheer impossibility. Slowly, slowly, however, we mount the narrow stair (the path is carefully made of loose stones in short zigzags), and after great labour the fjeld is attained. Then comes a walk over soft, snow-patched ground for a couple of miles ; then another farmhouse, with its creamy milk, served to us by a very wrinkled old woman. Now we see the distant peaks of the Halling Jokulen, covered with unbroken snows, glistening in the early morning sun.

At a little distance over rolling moorland of the fjeld, to our left, a light mist hangs in the air between us and a towering wall of rock ; it is the spray of the Voring Foss. Through thick undergrowth and a small wood of stunted birches we approach the river, that dashes on here as wildly and furiously as below the fall ; and following its course about ten minutes, the roar of the mighty waterfall gradually opens its ceaseless thunders upon us.

We see the Foss now in great force ; the melting snows and recent rains have largely increased the river's volume ; and, with a sublime unity of tremendous power and beauty, the waters sweep unbroken over the rocks, spreading themselves in their descent into a thick network of myriad-formed spray of purest white, and lashing into terrible action the affrighted pool beneath. The effect of the Voring

Foss is overwhelming. Gazing at the fearful height from which we see it, lying upon a ledge of rock sloping towards the chasm, it is awful to watch the boiling cauldron below, and to hear the vibrating thunder of that tremendous, sullen, and steady cannonade. These give us the crushing sense of power, while the simple outlines of the fall as a single column, woven into multitudinous beauties in its descent,—this, and the radiant iris hanging on the spray, are a source of perpetual beauty.

The height of this fall is variously estimated at from 800 to 1,000 feet; it is considered to be the grandest fall in Norway, and by some travellers said to be the finest in Europe.

We returned by the same path up which we had ascended, and in our descent from the fjeld had magnificent views of the truly Alpine valley down which the river flows from the Foss. The view from the head of this valley is sufficient reward to the traveller for the very considerable labour and fatigue, were there no waterfall as a consummation.

We arrived at Vik about one o'clock. A visit to the Voring Foss may therefore be made without discomfort in twelve hours from Vik. Here we were again driven to wretched coffee and a few eggs, with unpalatable bread; and at half-past one we took boat for Eide, on another branch of the Hardanger Fjord.

After fatigue, it is a most agreeable method of obtaining rest, to lie down, as is the custom here, upon the branches of birch strewn at the bottom of the boat. There is usually no seat provided for the passenger, and thus reposing we glided along the waters of the fjord.

The Hardanger has been called by one of the most cultivated of Norwegians, "The Paradise of Norway;" and the fjord certainly realised our highest imaginations of lake and mountain scenery. The main artery of the fjord is several miles in width, and the mountains at its head are of gigantic proportions, whilst, as they slope down to the water's edge, thick wood and frequent patches of cultivation give the finer features of a lake picture. At certain points, such as the opening vista of the Sor Fjord, where the mountain ranges of the Folgefonden, white with the snows of a thousand years, are clearly visible, the view is sublime.

As the afternoon advanced, the clouds, hitherto sailing grandly over the mountains, revealing depths of clear dark blue between, now hung heavily upon their summits; and here and there we saw heavy showers trailing along the mountain sides and across the fjord. By-and-by the sky changes into a thin grey veil, darkening rapidly into thick cloud, and rain descends. The water, hitherto calm, swells uneasily; and very speedily, as if agitated at the sudden change from light to darkness, rolls in huge broken waves. We are surrounded by thick mist; only the near shore of the fjord, which the boatmen hug so closely that their oars sometimes strike the rocks, is visible. The rain is now a deluge, and as it were for life the boatmen grimly work to keep our little skiff across the waves. Still the wind and rain increase, and the darkness deepens into thick night. The waves dash round us with an eager whirl, and our small craft strains and labours under the unusual pressure. It is a storm in the Hardanger; and to me a fearful scene. I confess that as I sat silently and anxiously watching the faces of the men, and the increasing violence of the water, which seemed to be lashing itself into the rage of desolation, I thought of many dear faces at home, and the possibilities of a long night for all of us. With a wish to work, if of any use, I asked whether there was any danger in the storm for us; but the boatman said "No:" we should make our destination that night; and I lay back in the foliage to await our deliverance.

In an hour or more the clouds broke asunder, light descended, the rain gradually ceased to fall, the wind softened down to a light breeze, a small sail was hoisted, and the boatmen, tired with their long labour, took out a quid and rested on their oars as we sped before the wind. The water, as rapidly as it had heaped itself, became calm and tranquil, and soon after ten o'clock we quietly and somewhat abruptly ran into Eide, at the head of the fjord.

Here we found excellent quarters, conducted by our boatmen, who seemed as thankful as ourselves to be once more upon the land, and in sight of food and rest. The station-master at Eide was a Dutchman; he understood not a word of English, and we very little Norsk, yet we never had a more hospitable reception. An excellent supper was quickly ready; all that tired travellers hoped for was to be had, and with much thankfulness and not a little fatigue, after about forty hours' almost incessant movement, we crept to our snug beds.

The station at Eide was a refreshing contrast to the empty cupboard to which we had been treated at Vik. We obtained excellent wine, and very superior cookery. Reindeer at breakfast, with consumable ham; and eggs, dressed with a fresh salad in most palatable style, attractively served by our "neat-handed Phyllis" of a hostess, crowned with the most piquant of little caps.

The weather brightening, we set off in good time, a short walk to Gravens Vand, the lake over which we were rowed yesterday on our way to the fjeld above Ulvik, and in about an hour we were at Over-Vassenden. Here I had been asked by the spokesman of a numerous crowd, very deferentially, whether I was a lord, to which I replied (with, I am afraid, a twinkle in my eye as I looked upon my friend waiting for me in the boat) in the language of an illustrious poet, "Lord of myself, this heritage of woe;" an answer which, as it appeared to indicate a long title, gave great satisfaction.

Throughout the long fifteen miles from Vassenden to Voss, the rain, which had begun whilst we were on the lake, continued without intermission. Not a thin drizzle, but unmistakably heavy wet, that penetrated and saturated the entire fabric in a very short time. We thus saw the same beautiful scenes through which we had walked so short a time ago, under a new aspect; and though less agreeable to us to plod along, plish, plash, through mire and wet, yet grandly impressive as another characteristic phase of Norwegian scenery.

In dripping plight we reached our old quarters at Voss, where we again had recourse to tea, the true elixir for pedestrians. By the kindness of our hostess I was accommodated with a large dressing gown, whose ample folds enabled me to move about the house *sans culotte* with perfect freedom and ease; and to attend upon my comrade in the same elegant condition, minus dressing gown. The cookery and refreshment here were good, and charges moderate; which, combined with good humour and hospitable dispositions, made the inn a sort of second home. We left with regret that our stay must necessarily be so short.

It was Sunday morning, the bell had tolled, and sailing across the calm lake came boats from several distant points carrying peasants to mass. We walked into the ancient church, and the choir-master thrilled our hearts with a few bars of divine melody, awakening blessed memories; and realising to me the noble words of our Lancashire poet—

"Sabbath, thou art the Ararat of life,
Smiling above the deluge of my cares."

The church is rather large, compared with many we had passed; it would hold several hundred people; there are pews, a gallery supported by curious twisted pillars, an altar, very primitive altar rails, curiously painted open roof, and a sweet toned organ made by the organist, quite a musical genius. The building is chiefly of wood, well pitched, and it seemed incredible to us that such a building should have withstood the winters of six hundred years.

The maidens, in their Sunday costume, the Bible folded within a clean napkin in hand, walk placidly in couples or groups into the church. They are very fair to look upon, with braided hair, long blue woollen skirts, and bodice of much ornament across the breast, with red and white sleeves. In and near the church we saw probably a hundred girls in this pretty guise. The men hung about the doors until near the time of mass. The maidens are distinguished by their dress from women, whose hair, we were told, is cut at marriage, and who wear no ornaments except on great occasions. This was a charming picture, and, hanging it about our hearts, we slowly and with frequent backward gaze left Voss. We were accompanied on our way a few miles by a gentleman resident, through whose kindness we had seen the church, and who, like most Norwegians we met, seemed anxious that we should see and know all to which they could help us.

From Voss the post road to Christiania winds along the mountain sides, commanding fine views of the rich valleys and lakes. Near us the mountains stretch upwards to an enormous height, and over the hills, across the valley, rise peak beyond peak, until the pine fringed height is lost in snow. The scenery increases in beauty as we ascend the vale; but though occasionally dipping, and sometimes shut in on all sides, the road is really for many miles up one great vale. About nine or ten miles from Voss, the river, wide and deep, forces itself through a very narrow cleft in the rock with a tremendous plunge, reminding one

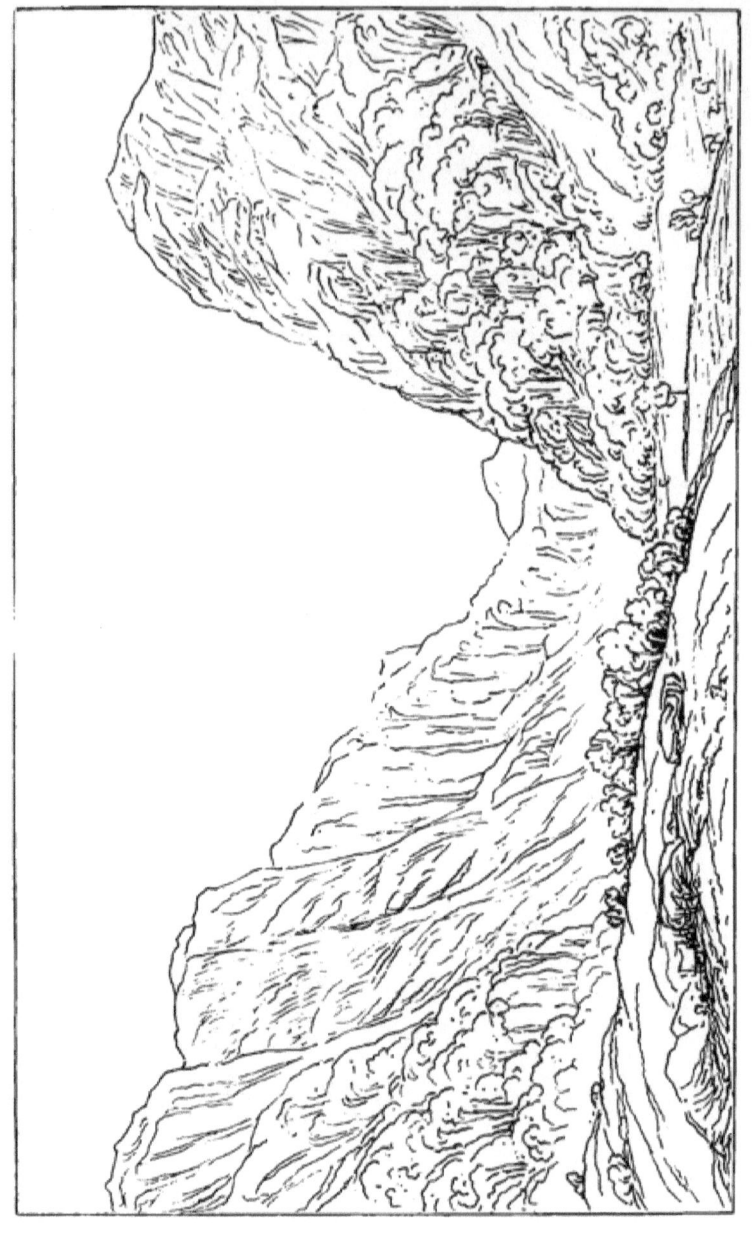

NAERODAL.

of the Strid, near Bolton Abbey, but of far vaster volume and of more fearful power. A few miles more and we are at the head of the valley, which we now see mapped out far below : a glorious sight,—wood, lake, foss, river, and hill mingled in harmonious combination.

Diverging from the highway, we seek the grassy bank of the mountain stream, and, after the fashion prescribed by Mattieu Williams, whose book on Norway everybody should read, commence our laundry work, followed by a stretch in the cooling stream,—the clear, cold water plashing over us as we recline in its shallow bed. Followed by a Turkish towel this is most refreshing. It gives vigour to the system, and supplements those sanitary requirements in regard to cleanliness of which there is so much need in Norway.

The road is now over high barren moorland ; we have lost our views of the valley and are in a basin of the mountains ; so, for several miles, gradually we are descending, and by-and-by we reach the head of a very deep and narrow valley, into which two large rivers leap. It is the head of the famed Nærodalen, and the plunging rivers form the two fine falls of the Sevelfos and the Stalemfos.

The descent into the Nærodalen is down a series of zigzags cut out of the rock, constructed with great skill, and rendered safe even for driving. From this road the two falls are seen by turns, one on either hand ; the river and road in graceful curves winding through the valley far below. The characteristics of Nærodalen are, its extreme narrowness, the great height of the mountains which enclose the defile, the great length to which it extends, and the variety of outline of its numerous rocks. They are variously estimated, and range from two to five thousand feet in height.

Near Nærodalen we had an unctuous draught of yellow milk, fresh from the cow, from two singular old women on the hill side, reminding us of the witches in Macbeth, by their strange garments and wrinkled skins. Milk, *ad libitum*, for eight skillings, and such milk ! We had previously sheltered during a passing shower at a farm on the road, thus obtaining a glimpse into the domestic arrangements of Norwegian farm life. The dog is a constant and noisy inmate ; he does not, however, show his teeth, he is " full of sound and fury." We there had beer and a sort of wine, Norwegian champagne, very pleasant to the taste, but highly charged with bowel-derangement ; rye-bread and butter ; with the incessant flad-brod, only taken when we could have nothing else. As we sat, a prettily dressed girl, whom we had passed on the road, entered, with psalm book and napkin in hand ; who, after walking straight to the table, sat and commenced eating out of a huge bowl (the common stock, which a man had left as we went in) the peculiar porridge of the country ; eating it with a large wooden spoon, quite placidly, and as a matter of course. The spoon is an institution ; each person has one, and when they have finished the meal it is carefully licked, and placed in a small niche, awaiting further use.

The mand (husband) and knone (wife) were very nice people ; they had about them several children, and one of the grandmothers, who lay abed watching us with the rest of the group, as we sat at meat. The gudeman read a little Norsk to us, which I could not follow, from a book on domestic cookery, containing the recipe for the wine. He also showed me a large Norsk Bible, from which we had further reading. It is the common custom to have beds in every room ; there were two where we sat, in the kitchen, and I observed elsewhere that at least children are put to bed perfectly nude.

The fire-place is just an open hearth, with the usual iron suspender for pans, or a huge cauldron, as required. Birch is burnt for fire-wood ; each house has its stack prepared. Payment here was left with us entirely, and a mark caused much expression of feeling. Shaking of the hand always accompanies anything given, with the expression " Mange tak " (many thanks). The appearance of two Englishmen everywhere almost creates a little sensation : it is to be hoped that this pleasant feeling will be perpetuated by further intercourse. We had another debauch upon milk, by-the-way, in the morning (after our bathe), in the presence of a considerable village crowd ; and upon asking what we had to pay, were told, after a consultation behind the door of the house, one skilling (less than a halfpenny) ! I think this outdoes anything I have known.

Our walk through the Nærodalen was the crowning enjoyment of a long day's walk, full of beauty and interest ; and it served to quicken our relaxing steps, and to relight the almost sated eye. The walk along the dale is nearly level, rich grass and patches of cultivation

NÆRÖDAL.

STALHEIM FOSS.

NEAR GUDVANGEN.

skirting the road. The river, flowing down the centre, fed by many cascades, and several important streams, besides the two waterfalls at the head of the vale, swells to a considerable volume ere it plunges into the fjord, about eight miles below. The mountains—rugged, wild, pine-covered, snow-capped, barren, or streaked with many-coloured lichens and dark moss—tower on either hand, in every conceivable variety of outline, and always lofty, requiring the head to be thrown back to catch their summits. Here and there, immense heaps of rock that have been detached from the mountain side almost block the path, and huge boulders, like stranded ships, are frequent. Seen as we saw the Nærodalen, with a setting sun, and in twilight, it became sombre and gloomy near the end; but a grander or more impressive embodiment of the overwhelming majesty of nature I have never beheld.

As we approach Gudvangen, many goats were near the lower shelves of rock, and in the green meadows, sweet, clean, small cows browsed on the delicious herbage.

The station of Gudvangen, to which we had looked forward as to a Goshen out of our wilderness of fatigue, proved a sad disappointment; for though Murray and Mr. Williams speak of it as "good," we found the food poor and badly cooked; the house ill-ventilated, the stationmaster a boor, and the charges high. Bad fare and high charges often go together.

The Næro Fjord is a prolongation of Narrow Valley, or *vice versâ*. The same character of towering rocks, striking sheer downwards thousands of feet, perpendicularly almost, to the waters of the fjord. Along this we took boat; it was an exciting sail, each slight turn giving us a fresh combination of form, by grouping the mighty masses into new pictures. Many waterfalls throw themselves headlong down from these heights, and besides the Keel Foss, at Gudvangen, of which much is said in Murray and others, we noticed with more admiration the Haaberg Foss and the Sagel Foss as very grand. Possibly these are less fine in the middle of summer, when the snows have passed away, and the weather is dry. A couple of hours, or a little more, brought us into the great Sogne Fjord, of which the Næro Fjord is but a very short arm.

The sail along the Sogne Fjord is wonderfully beautiful, the vast expanse of calm water, the loftier mountains and distant snow peaks, came in continual variety, as we moved slowly by the shores.

At Groningen we paused about a quarter of an hour, and, by the hospitality of a gentleman residing on the rocks, had an excellent luncheon.

The fjord here expands, forming a magnificent lake; much wood on the hills near us, but too rocky for further cultivation. The distant mountain, though snow-covered, seems to be very beautiful at its base, clothed with verdure and sunshine. The rocks here are very friable with constant cleavage, sometimes breaking away in fragments of immense size. Still grander mountain views, as we approach the entrance of the fjord to Lierdalsoren, the water less broad, and evidently running up into the land. At six o'clock we made the quaint little town of Lierdalsoren, after a pull of about ten hours, with very little rest. The charge for this long ride, for three boatmen and boat, including drikke-penge (drink money), was three dollars and three marks.

As we approached Lierdalsoren, it seemed like a collection of toy houses, cut out of cardboard and painted in bright colours. The houses, all of wood, are small, and the mountain at the foot of which the town is built so lofty, that the whole town, seen from a distance, appears like a few large pegs or stumps at the margin of the fjord; and when one gets ashore, it is all so miniature that one may easily fancy it a theatrical stage, and the foregoing sail over the fjord a pleasant dream. Here this illusion was heightened and momentarily confirmed after we had sat down in the station by the sound of a distant drum, like the rat, tat, tat, in " Figlia del Reggimento." We rub our eyes; yes, here it comes; two drums and a regiment of soldiers; the whole thing seems to have been " got up." They march past, "halt, right about face," a short harangue, and they are dismissed, dispersing rapidly behind the scenes. The old-fashioned muskets and bayonets, the cumbrous bearskin knapsacks, heavily strapped and hanging loosely about the back; their helmets, the large coats on small men and the small coats on large men, with trousers ditto; and the general supernumerary appearance of the entire force, half militia, half line, certainly justified our first laughable view.

STÜVE; ON NAERO FJORD.

Entrance to Naero Fjord.

NAERO FJORD.

The station at Lierdalsoren is the best we have seen in Norway; pleasant commodious rooms, scrupulously clean, with longer beds; for the Norwegian beds are so short that you always awake with your knees forming the apex of a pyramid; and if the people are not generally smaller than ourselves, they must coil themselves in their sleep. The best Rhine wine is here two marks twelve skillings a bottle; and excellent malt liquor at a fraction under fivepence for a full pint bottle, quite equal to Bass or Allsopp. It is quite time that the malt duty should go.

After tea, at which we had superb salmon, fresh from his native element, and potatoes, which are almost invariably served morning, noon, and night, we sauntered about the town, looking into one or two shops. The "apothek" here has evidently a large business; his shop is the largest in the place, well stocked with the usual array of bottles, and, as it is the post office, affords a pleasant opportunity for acquiring a little Norsk, and gratifying our legitimate curiosity at the same time. Over the door of the baker's shop, both here and at Bergen, I noticed a curious sign, like a piece of twisted cable, thus ∞.

At several places we met with bread made into this shape but it is hard and dry. A few tin pans, a general provision establishment, a kind of "store" for things in general, with a small warehouse on the little wooden quay, formed the business section of Lierdal; whilst the station, a few large houses, the telegraph office, and a military establishment constitute the semi-suburban element. It is all in miniature, and, placed on a flat, surrounded by mountains not far apart, looks really most insignificant. There were, however, nearly two hundred soldiers here, including militia, and recruiting appeared to be going on briskly. There were about half-a-dozen of the officers staying at the station, who politely asked us to join their table at dinner the next day, and though all conversation was by means of a combination of English, Norsk, and French, I do not remember for many a day to have passed so cheerful an hour. We drank to Gamlé Norge, and our Norwegian friends toasted "Old England" with genuine hurrahs, such as I had thought before could only have been heard at home. They are a fine hearty people, and so far as we have experienced, love the English.

On the shore of the fjord, near the little quay, were many boats, undergoing the usual annual overhauling for the summer season. The boatmen of the Sogne and Hardanger Fjords are a hardy race. Six, eight, and ten hours of almost uninterrupted rowing we had several times (in the Hardanger, with a heavy sea), as I have related. A quid of tobacco whilst at work; and during the short intervals for eating, flad-brod, raw bacon, and sour milk in large quantities, are their nourishment and stimulants on the water; and our experience would justify the conclusion that they are sober, honest, and cheerful. The Hardanger boatmen all wear a knife; in the Sogne Fjord I did not observe any.

From Lierdalsoren we took boat to Ronnei, at the head of the Gaupne Fjord, a remote ramification of the great Sogne Fjord. It is a distance of about 28 miles. This was pulled over in about six hours, including the short stoppage for dinner. Our boatmen were hearty fellows, rowing with the regularity of a machine, with lively chat, and the occasional humming of a Norwegian air. The youngest of these men was 29 years old, a strapping man of six feet; the others beyond middle age—one 54, the eldest 61, but he strong and vigorous, and apparently with a score of years' good work in his sinewy arms.

It is a magnificent sail across this part of the Sogne Fjord. The distant mountains are of great height—four, five, and six thousand feet, topped with unbroken snow, while those contiguous to the lake are often covered with thick pine forests.

As we sail along a reach of the fjord we catch grand views of the sombre Aardals Fjord and the far-distant peaks of the Horungerne range of mountains, the loftiest in Norway. Turning into the Lyster Fjord, we shortly pass Solvorn, beautifully situated on a curve of the mountain. Its bright green patches of corn field and meadow, the red tiled, whitewashed station, and a thin line of road traced up the centre of the ascending valley, contrast agreeably with the near rugged mountain sides and broad background of snow. At each turn hereabouts the latest seems the best, and grander scenes to expand. We are nearing the loftiest ranges, and the fjords narrow as they pass into the valleys. Soon we turn into the Gaupne Fjord, and passing Marifjoren, most picturesquely straggling up a gentle acclivity, come upon Ronnei, as the setting sun lights up the mountain heights on the opposite shore with golden fire.

It is a calm, clear summer night. The orange tints linger on the mountain tops, and every hill and rock is sharply defined against the light blue heaven. A solitary star shines faintly in the western sky, the birds still gently sing; the air is very still; the rich golden glow is no more, but soft twilight rests upon the scene, and we feel that the spirit of beauty has passed over the earth. It is nearly eleven o'clock, as I write, in the Ronnei station, looking out of our little room upon this calm picture, yet sufficiently light, and pleasantly warm.

Shortly after this, the Skyds-skaffer entered to say that our horses were ready, and we started on our excursion up the Justedalen. The road, alongside the clear river which flows down the valley, is, after the first mile or two, very irregular and broken. As we advance up the vale, giant rocks on either hand cast down their vast shadows upon the twilight, and for a short time we experience the gloom of night. In the stillness of the woods, as we move quietly along, the horses feeling their way over the rough stones, the rushing river is the only voice, and he sings an exciting song. From the far off snows and fields of ice he hurries wildly to the warm and sheltered fjord.

The path shortly crosses a hill that almost blocks up the valley, covered with thick wood; yet as we come upon little openings in the forest, we see the immense rocks above us, and occasionally the path is traced upon the edge of the hill, overhanging the roaring river, and we look down upon frightful depths. It is extremely grand. Now we descend into a long flat, in which are two or three farms, with much cattle and numerous goats. The river is very noisy here. From one of these green luscious patches we see, as we look up towards the western sky, a thin line of red fire resting on the snow,—Earth's crimson blush, awakened by the Morn. In the east thin lines of bright red vapour float high in the heavens. A flush of deeper yellow comes throbbing up behind the hill, and with radiant pulsation,

"Day, like a mighty river, rushes in."

Still our small cavalcade moves on, now deep in the dale in the shadow of vast rocks, wildly fantastical; now climbing a steep path through darkened woods, thick with luxuriant growth of loftiest pines. We are moving amidst the indescribable sublimities of nature, and, in the presence of this manifestation of God, gaze with eager yet reverential eye. The hours advance, and, as the morning sun rises to flood his light across the vale, vapour and thick cloud strive for the mastery. It is almost cold, and we begin to fear the clouds. We have now reached the Præstegaard and church of the Justedal, about twenty-one miles from Ronnei. It is nearly six o'clock. The good rector of this remote parish is very kind, and we are soon in the enjoyment of his hospitality. Coffee is set before us. Upon coming into the house for repose we discover that we are very cold, and feel that the loss of rest and the long ride are matters of hard dry fact, not to be shirked. At the pressing suit of the good man, I turn in for a couple of hours' sleep. Wisely recommended. Punctually to the time, we are called by our host; but, alas! to what a change of scene. No sun, no sky, no distant snow-clad mountains; only the dimly looming masses of mountain and rock that form the outer walls of this great valley. Thick clouds lie heavily over head, and along the hills drag white vapours, drifting lower and lower; the rain is falling furiously, and our horses are shivering at the door.

One great object of our visit to the Justedal was to see the Nygaard glacier, one of the largest in Norway, about nine or ten miles higher up the valley. After much anxious deliberation and advice from the Rector, whose decided opinion was that to go on would yield nothing but fatigue, we determined upon a return. We visited the church or "temple," as the good priest called it, a most primitive little place, the pews and other woodwork painted most fantastically red and black. On the tiny altar were two or three half-burned thick tallow candles, and some half-dozen common wine bottles. Everything was of the very rudest description, eloquent of its isolated situation. Yet even to this remote and unfrequented spot, the great tidings of the noble Garibaldi's work had been carried; and the manly grip with which the good pastor shook our hands, and literally danced with delight about the room when we told him that Palermo was in the patriot's possession, was deeply affecting. It was an experience I shall never forget, and shall always look back upon with feelings of deeper gratitude to God and love to man.

We reached Ronnei in the afternoon, somewhat dispirited, very wet and fagged, but impressed with the marvellous grandeur of the Justedalen. At Ronnei station, the Interlachen of our ramble, we received the most considerate attention, and cannot speak too warmly of the quiet, unobtrusive manner of the people. The material comforts of a footbath, daintily wrought slippers, nicely cooked game and aromatic coffee, with the higher hearteasing enjoyments of cheerful voices and kind tranquil faces, gave our imaginations full license for the belief that this evening was an hour's Norwegian dream. The next morning early we resumed our boat ; the same men who had brought us having bargained with us to have the return fare ; and after another delicious six hours' ride, reached our late pleasant quarters at Lierdalsoren.

During the afternoon, we shouldered our knapsacks once more, and trudged on from Lierdal, pausing a few minutes to watch the evolutions of the military on parade. We walked along the valley of the Lierdals Elv, which appears to have been in remote ages a continuation of the fjord, and is even now, for a considerable distance, very little elevated above the level of the water. Accumulations of earth, in terrace-like mounds, also indicate a past era of deeper water. As we penetrate the valley, the road ascends, and even after the wondrous Justedalen, is yet grand and exciting. We had a very pleasant walk to Lysne, about eight or nine miles from Lierdalsoren ; and here we made acquaintance with the genuine roadside Norwegian station. It was a small farm, a short way off the road, with nothing to mark its special character ; and we should have passed by, but a lad, with the return mail cart (four-wheeled and small), whose acquaintance we made on the road, took us there.

The apartment for travellers was small, well lighted (all the houses in Norway have plenty of light, with few curtains), and, quite an exceptional occurrence, we found the windows open. In the room were the bed, several wooden-seated chairs, a cupboard, painted in a curious grotesque style, red and white ; a looking-glass, and stove. The walls, ceiling, and floor, of bare deal boards. We found excellent beer, and a loaf of sweet rye bread. On these we supped, deciding to remain for the night. The weather looked threatening, a rising wind, with much cloud surging wildly round the mountain heights. Opposite to the window at which I sat was a fine foss—a single stream, dashing over a ledge of rock, with a clear fall of probably 200 feet or more— the Hoa Foss, not noticed in the guide books, but sufficiently beautiful to make the fortunes of half a dozen innkeepers if in Cumberland, North Wales, or Devon.

I do not remember any book of travel in Norway that omits to mention, either prominently or otherwise, the perpetual annoyance from fleas and a more disagreeable creature; and I had hoped from our experience to have been able, in a limited circle, to have corrected what began to appear to be a national prejudice and delusion. But my comrade, upon casually turning down the sheets at an early hour, called my attention to the fact that the Philistines would soon be upon us if we went to bed; so we began to consider how to sleep without "going to bed." Luckily, the table had two huge laps, and placing our knapsacks as pillows, we rolled ourselves in our plaids, and without undressing, stretched at full length upon the table, were soon asleep.

We awoke at an early hour, and after very limited lavations, doubled up our bed, and took a quiet hour or two at these hastily written notes. It was a wet morning; we had still a piece of the previous night's loaf; with this and a cup of tea we made our breakfast.

Upon asking for a further supply of bread (butter was evidently a myth), we found there was nothing in the house but one old loaf, like a brick, which the woman, with a doubtful smile, produced. It was clearly time to be moving, though still very wet and darkly threatening. We paid our modest bill of a mark and a half (1s. 4d.), and trudged on.

The rain continued, somewhat interfering with our enjoyment of the fine scenery of this valley, which is highly attractive—of a like character, as to broad outline, to the Justedal, although not so grand. At Husum, the rain increasing, we obtained horses and the carts of the country—small wooden things, without springs, that shake your interior viscera in excruciating style. With these we pushed along, ascending rapidly towards Haeg by zig-zags, skilfully constructed on the mountain face.

NEAR HUSUM.

NEAR HUSUM.

NEAR BORGUND.

On this stage we passed the most singular old church of Borgund, with its quaint and separate bell tower. It stands a little distance from the road, in the flat meadows of the valley, and is one of the most interesting buildings in Norway, entirely of wood, and certainly not less than six or seven hundred years old. Its appearance is a combination of the Chinese pagoda, with the Eastern mosque, and our "early English" cathedrals. Sir Charles Anderson, in his interesting journal, has written an able description, and gives an outline sketch of considerable merit.

The rain was so heavy, with a violent and increasing wind, that our stay here was very brief. As we jogged on, the river was foaming down the valley, and the mountain streams, tearing down from their lofty sources, literally filled the air with the noise of many waters. At Haeg we changed horses, just peeping into the station, a much better house than the one at Husum, from which we had been conducted by a most brigand looking personage.

The next stage, Haeg to Maristuen, was a scene of wild grandeur; the roaring river, now swollen and lashed into the fury of a mountain torrent, came with terrible force and reality past us as we drove excitedly along. As we ascended the approaches to the Fille Fjeld the waters were still more furious, the rain falling in a stream. Here and there the torrents from the hills had crossed the road, and the river was fast rising to within a few inches from the top of its rock-bound limits. The moors and mountains were covered with driving mist and a thick heavy canopy of clouds. As we neared Maristuen the road was cut up with a mountain torrent, and we waded up to the horse's knees ; and a little beyond this point, and down an incline in the road, the water had rushed from the hills, and was tearing up the post road, making it into a water-course. As our horses strained over the upheaved stones, and the dashing water rushed by up to our axles, it was navigating rather than driving, and I began to realise the fearful effects of a storm on the bleak heights to which we were going. At last, wet and weary, we arrived at Maristuen, where we found the house topsy-turvy from the flood. The inmates from the surrounding dwellings had come for shelter here, bringing with them their bedding, and even here the rain was in several places pouring through the roof. There were some twenty souls assembled in this house, the only shelter from the unabating storm. Here in the warm, stove-heated, common room we sat and took tea, contributing much to the amusement of the various members of the motley group, who were curious to watch how Englishmen did the simplest things; and chattering as far as we were able, aided by looks and gesture, we felt most thoroughly, "One touch of nature makes the whole world kin." During the long night "the rain descended and the floods came and beat against that house." Fortunately for all of us, it was founded upon a rock, and a little sheltered by neighbouring undulations that broke the rude shock of the wind, and turned the water currents aside. In the early morning we saw that the force of the storm had been spent, by the decreased volume of water rushing along the almost river-road. We therefore ordered horses, carriole, and cart, and in the rain once more pushed on (encased now in oilskins and waterproofs, lent to us by the good people here), towards Nystuen, on the Fille Fjeld.

The scenery was extremely wild, with long stretches of moorland; now a wide uncultivated valley, with a few sæters far apart; now the road rises on to the hill side, dotted with stunted and gnarled birch trees, scarcely yet in leaf. The reindeer moss lies here in thick clumps, and many-coloured lichens paint the rocks. As we have dashed forward, the rain has gradually ceased to fall, and a gleam of sunshine lights up the vast plateau of the Fille Fjeld, the great patches of snow on every side glistening in the bright and glancing light. It is still blowing hard, and the rain dashes occasionally in our faces as we drive along the undulating wilds. By-and-by we are met by two men, who speak to the driver of the cart in advance, with serious faces, looking toward the mountain side before us. There is evidently something of very grave import. The driver says that we cannot proceed,—that water floods the road. But we persist, and at length move on again, one of the men coming with us. Now the road is covered with water, but the stones on each side, and the poles of the telegraph, which is carried overland from Christiana to Bergen, sufficiently indicate its whereabouts; so, venturing almost up to the horses' girths, we pass safely over. If that is all, what a fuss, we think, and away we drive another mile or so. Then the driver gets off and

BORGUND CHURCH.

resolutely ties up his reins, and says he shall go on no more. The mountain side has come down with the force of the flood, and, crossing the road, has ploughed it up, carrying earth and rocks and trees before it; and for thirty or forty yards what was the road is a heap of rocks and mud water-courses. Still, we wish to go forward, and, a strong man taking our knapsacks on his back, we scramble carefully over the broken rocks and *débris*, following the steps of our guide, who, with long staff, cautiously feels his way.

A short distance, and the same havoc is before us again, and yet again, before we arrive at the station, which is not more than a mile from where we left our carrioles. At length we reach the Nystuen station, a comfortable place; the hale old man who carries our "traps," and who has piloted us across the wrecks, is the station master.

He relates to us how terrible a night he has had; no sleep, but saddest anticipations. On each side his house, at a short distance, one of these fearful descents from the mountains had rushed down, threatening to sweep houses and every living thing into the lake just below the road. "Ah! it was frightsome," said he; "at seven last night that came down, and at three this morning that other great torrent," pointing to the one we had last crossed.

How thankful I am that we have escaped these dangers; may we be preserved from any that are in the future!

By the old man's counsel we have remained here all day, hoping that the road will be less soft to-morrow after the sun and wind of this morning. It has been very promising all day; but now, at seven o'clock, the wind is again south-west, and the rain is heavy. As I write and look out of the window I can count the track of five of those sweeping destructive mountain torrents over whose desolations we shall have to scramble; and our old friend tells us there will be many more as we go down, as they would have the storm still heavier on the other side.

The scene here, apart from the recent events, is one of the sheerest desolation. Snow is all around us in very thick patches; the sky is leaden dull; no vegetation clothes the mountains—they are almost barren rocks; and here, in the bosom of these solitudes, is a wide lake, almost covered with massive ice.

Within doors, however, the picture is more cheerful. My friend sits writing, at the same table, opposite to me; we have our maps and books about us, and have had some hours of quiet indoor pleasures. On one side the room are two nice beds, clean and tidy; a washing table, &c., in the corner; several homely chairs, and a small square table, at which we dined, and to which we shall shortly adjourn for tea. At my elbow, on the wall, is a portrait of our hostess, a nice motherly woman; and over her is an engraving of Her Most Gracious Majesty Victoria, by the grace of God, Queen. There is also, against the wall, a rather handsome mirror, for these remote regions, and at my back a fantastically painted three-cornered cupboard. We are each in our shirt sleeves, and without shoes. I have not undergone the "domestic surgery" of a shave for several days, and I discarded braces for a strap round the waist a fortnight ago. Neckties and collars are nearly obsolete. At the other end of the room is a large stove, in which we have lighted a good fire, and arranged round it on chairs are our coats and plaids. On lines of thick twine, artistically constructed, we have suspended our shirts, stockings, and pocket handkerchiefs; whilst, in the centre, from the ceiling, like a joint of meat, or a clock pendulum, hangs my felt hat, that at an early hour this morning was reduced to the consistency of a soft oatmeal cake. In a row, like an advanced guard to this army of rags, are placed our boots and shoes, well greased or oiled for the expected rain of to-morrow. As I write this picture, another feature is added to the room; the maiden enters, and is now busily employed in arranging the beds and bedding for the night. She is dressed more like an English girl than is usual here, and not nearly so picturesque a subject as her mother, who is going about in a pair of bright scarlet stockings and short petticoats, with braided hair and blue bodice.

After a few hours' uneasy sleep I rose, about three o'clock, to the gloomy prospect of heavy rain, which continued incessantly until about six o'clock.

The good old skaffer found us a strong man to assist in carrying our knapsacks, and about seven o'clock we started the descent, our old friend giving us his heartiest good wishes, and gazing long after us. By taking a boat along the edge of the lake, across the surface of which the ice had been drifted by the wind during the night to the other end, we escaped the crossing of two or three of the "screyas" nearest to Nystuen. The clouds slowly lifted, and occasional breaks showed some slight promise of fair weather. As we slowly descended from the fjeld, the rocks uplifted their dark and jagged peaks, and the scene that unfolded before us was one of wild, desolate grandeur. The snow, at a short walk from Nystuen, spread across the road, and we frequently came upon patches, six or eight feet thick, winding along the hollows like small glaciers. As we descended into the deep valley, whose river is one channel for the waters from the immense area of these vast fjelds, the extent of the storm was slowly disclosed. The road was quite impassable. We had given up considering the number of mere obstructions from fallen rocks and earth, for the water had overflowed its usual bounds, covering the road deeply, and we were obliged to ascend the mountain side, and scramble through the woods. This was repeated several times. Still lower down in the valley, on the opposite side to that on which we walked, were several villages, and from the heights above them the rain had poured in such a deluge as to bring away masses of the mountain side, ploughing into it deep furrows, and spreading desolation and terror in its way. The river had become a vast yellow lake, with a tumultuously heaving current through its centre, trees and broken wood, the remains of the bridge across the valley, floating upon its surface.

Huge banks of mud and stones surrounded the dwellings, where patches of corn and bright green meadows had smiled in the sunshine but a day or two ago. Here and there the ruins of a little cluster of houses thrust themselves out of the *debris*. Over the valley, with looks of complete helplessness, wandered men and women, some in search of their scattered herds, and others gazing with hopeless looks upon the desolate scene. As we passed the little farms alongside our road, the man would stop to say a word or two to the women who came forward to the gate, and the rough faces trembled with emotion as they looked into each other's tearful eyes. It was most melancholy. Sadly and silently we walked, and in sight of that dreadful calamity and human suffering, I wondered how the sun could shine.

Still lower down the vale, and on the shores of a lake, great patches of the mountain side, with acres of pine forest, had slid down and been washed away in the tremendous storm. The telegraph poles, hitherto, as it were by a marvel, uninjured, were at this point carried away, and the wire, for a long distance, twirled like horsehair. At Quamme, three or four miles from the scene of the greatest havoc, the stone bridge had been carried away ; and on the opposite shores of the Lille Mjosen Vand, besides the destruction of many houses, cattle, and much property, several persons were overwhelmed by the mountain streams, and drowned.

From Quamme, we slowly scrambled, with a man to carry our small baggage, until near Thume, through scenes of beauty and grandeur that, under less painful conditions and feelings, would have been most enjoyable.

At a small farm in the woods, under the shadow of immense rocks, loftier than Snowdon, and almost precipitous at their summits, we obtained refreshment of rich milk, with flad-brod, for three persons, surrounded by the cheerful faces of a large and wondering family, as we sat upon a ledge of moss-carpeted rock. At our departure, I asked the man what we must pay him, and, after a little delay, took from my pocket a handful of coin, and requested him to help himself, purposely placing the larger pieces nearest to him. He took a four skilling piece (2d. value), and walked with us a quarter of a mile to point out the way. When I first entered the cottage he had the big old Bible before him on the table ; it was Sunday.

Near Thume we met with a boatman, who took us over the lake to Oyloe. As we sailed over the water, gusts of hot air blew in our faces, dark clouds quickly gathered, and a heavy thunderstorm broke over the hills ; the lightning glancing on the mountain peaks, with the bellowing thunder, adding to our melancholy sympathy for the poor villagers we had left behind us, and contributing not a little to our own personal anxiety.

At Oyloe we found, as the handbook faithfully records, "a wretched house ; " but, weary and sad, we were glad to find ourselves under any shelter. The hopelessness of getting home in our limited time here seemed to get the better of us, and our spirits were depressed with the dismal prospect. A lake behind us, the road frequently flooded and occasionally submerged, and another bridge broken down within sight on the only road before us. Our only way out of this dilemma, we were informed, was over the pine-covered hills on the other side of the water. The station master promised to find for us in the morning a boat, and two men to undertake our knapsacks and guide us. And with such hard fare as the place afforded, we went to bed, but scarcely to sleep. For, in addition to our anxieties, the fleas, &c., here re-visited us; and let philosophers teach transcendentalism as they please, the senses are absolute.

I made intimate acquaintance here with the whole house; it was dirty and slovenly everywhere. The mistress, a woman about forty, had been good-looking, but faded, and given, I am afraid, to stimulating drinks, which was the secret of all the disorder and discomfort. The man seemed decent and respectable—I was sorry for him. They had six children; the eldest, a lad of seventeen, sharp, intelligent, and good-looking. Not a single clean piece of crockery in the house, not a pan but required washing, not a crumb of wholesome bread to set before us. There were two loaves, thick with rich green mould, which the woman assured us were good *inside*, and proceeded to pare. I saw her wipe the teacups on the lap of a shirt hanging to dry before the fire, and wipe a knife upon the corner of her dirty dress. Two small pigs nestled in the kitchen nook, and a naked little urchin coiled himself upon a chair before the fire. The water for our tea was boiled in a small cauldron which imparted a flavour unknown to the same package of tea, either at Voss or elsewhere. The eggs, of course, were clean; but the spoons! We here, for the first time, used our own — (we had taken with us knife, fork, and spoon). How so ill-conducted a place is allowed to remain a station, and practise its extortions upon travellers—for the price of all this was more than at the best stations in Norway—is a matter of astonishment.

On Monday morning, about six o'clock, accompanied by the master and his son, we left the station at Oyloe, with thankfulness. We crossed the lake and walked several miles through forest, over broken, wet, and undulating ground, until we reached the highroad at a point only two miles from where we had set out. The bright sunny morning, the rich odours of the woods, and the spring of hope welling up within at the prospect of deliverance made this walk delicious; and as we stepped upon the post road once more, with the assurance that the waters were passed, a thrill of gratitude passed over me, and I silently wept.

Passing a small Niagara fall on our way, we came to Ste, where we obtained food, and shelter for a short time. Two students from Christiania, young athletes, called here (even they had been driven to carts by the weather), and we took their return car, a delightful drive up and down hill to Rein, the next station.

From Rein we pushed on towards Strands, but ere we had made half the distance were informed that the roads were again impassable, the clouds had again gathered thickly, and in a very short time we were driving through a heavy thunderstorm, the lightning playing vividly in quick succession, with thunder heavily reverberating. Awhile we sought the shelter of a log hut (common near the roads), the poor horse trembling with terror as each successive peal of thunder rattled overhead. Again the gleam of promise, so often unfulfilled, and we were jogging on our way. Another stoppage, another pause, another boat; when, by way of combining his own advantage with the lift he meant to favour us with in his own good time, the solitary boatman, at the bawling demand of a piratical fellow ashore, pulled out into the middle of the lake to fish and string together several timbers, which were slowly drifting away. After carefully securing them with a cord, he coolly towed them after us to the shore, and then, first landing his pirate friend, he took us on our way.

The station at Strands, where we landed, is on the edge of a lake, or inland fjord. It is an excellent, well-conducted house, ruled by quite a motherly woman, who cared for our wants, and took delight in ministering to them; with sufficiently unsophisticated nature to charge a just sum, to which her husband, a sharply qualified business man, added, with singular felicity, a large percentage. By this energetic skaffer and the aid of a Norwegian gentleman (staying in the house), who could read English, our further progress was expedited; and we again took boat to a point upon the lake, at which horse and car would meet us to carry us to Frydenlund, our destination for the night.

This was a fine drive along the mountain side, commanding extensive views of the long valley, the Strands Fjord, and its numerous islands, like another St. Lawrence, with the lofty, distant fjelds. At Frydenlund we had to rouse the house, but found very comfortable quarters.

The next morning our friend, the rain, was as lively as ever, the air cooler, and the road soft and splashy. Tired with the sixteen or seventeen hours' incessant work of the previous day, we did not get fairly under weigh until near ten o'clock.

The road still ascending, we had, in the intervals from rain and storm, magnificent views of the valley, lit up by occasional sun gleams; the fjord still at our feet, embosomed in thickly-wooded hills. In fairer weather, with clearer skies and dry skins, this must be as beautiful to look upon as any scene in Norway; and seen, as it is sometimes, from an elevation over which we had to climb—like an episode in our long day's poem—as high and toilsome to attain as Snowdon, it must be at sunset or sunrise sublime.

With us it was, in another respect, like what the ascent of Snowdon or Ben Nevis too frequently results in—a sojourn in the clouds. True, we sometimes caught these ever-wonderful and beautiful effects of light displayed by the moving mists uplifting momentarily, like a curtain, but these magical peeps into a heaven below us were "few and far between."

A couple of miles or so over the pass, as we descended into the next valley, the fringe of cloud was lifted, and we were shown a lovely picture, fresh from the Divine Artist's touch. Bathed in sunlight lay a richly-wooded valley, deep and broad, dotted with human dwellings, a spire-crowned church in the midst. Up the finely-sweeping braes grew thick pine forests, dark with massive foliage, and lofty as the clouds. A thin line of white, curved by the Mightiest Hand, waved through the vale, its liquid music mingling with the sighing woods, and reaching even the heights from which we looked. Into this loveliness we descended, and from thence looked back upon the steeps from whence we came, still fringed with trailing mists and dripping cloud. At Bruyflat we change horses, and rush on along the now almost level road to Tomlevold, a large station, quite a hostelry, with numerous outbuildings and large belfry. Again we are on the road, pass the exercise platz, where Norwegian irregulars are being drilled in the goose step—a step taken, alas, too prematurely by so sad a number of our fellow-creatures. On to Skoyen, another good comfortable station. We feel that we are approaching the confines of civilisation. We have actually just passed a dress coat on the road. What a guy he looked ! We are beginning to feel excited, as if we were almost at home, and our labours over ; for we have felt the last day or two that we are working hard, almost like sailing against wind and tide, to make a port.

At Skoyen, during the change of horses, we obtained what we thought excellent, and what I hope the reader will not consider at this time stale, beer ; and during the day we had comforted the inner man at Bruyflat, with the flutte milk of Norway (an invaluable discovery I owed to my friend), of which we largely skimmed the cream. It is the milk set aside for cheese, and is brought in large pails, with a top cream half an inch thick, and a layer of custard-like milk beneath ; this is eaten with sugar, and is as palatable as it is highly nutritive.

From Skoyen we took horses again and trotted on towards Lien. This and the last three are all fast stations. A mile or more out of Skoyen, an extensive prospect opened before us. The noble Rands Fjord, calmly beautiful, reposing in the sheltered bosom of swelling hills. As we climbed the hills, this view of the Rands Fjord and the far-stretching valley of the Strands Fjorden beyond, with the snowy peaks of loftiest fjelds far away in the distance, the setting sun and the gathering masses of broken cloud filling the western heavens, showed us the characteristic beauties of eastern Norwegian scenes in sharp contrast to the grander and more vast masses of rock and water of the western coast. As a picture of quiet, placid, tranquil beauty, I think this prospect of the Rands Fjord by sunset was perhaps the finest we had looked upon, during what seemed to us to be our long travels here. To those who have leisure, and can afford the time, it must be a great delight to begin at Christiania, and thus by almost imperceptible degrees grow from the quiet undulations amidst which we have now arrived into those mighty gigantic forms and groupings which culminate in the Alpine sublimities of the Fille Fjeld and the

Justedal. Yet with us it was exceedingly beautiful to feel ourselves descending into regions where the amenities of life were to be enjoyed, and to the prospect of once more coming to sit by the side of and look on the faces of our friends at home.

At Lien, we changed horses for Mustaed, and drove for an hour or more along a newly-constructed level road, through thick fir plantations.

The station at Mustaed is of a very superior style to most that we have seen. It is nearer the capital, and a place of resort in summer for the Christiania people. Here we concluded to have a day's rest before entering Christiania, so as to be able to enjoy with freshness of body and mind the sight of so interesting a section of our plan. The interiors here are painted with delicate tints, with great care and in excellent taste. The rooms are large, well ventilated; flooded with light, as I have before observed is the case generally in Norway. It is a large farm, and in the great yard, an acre at least in extent, are two huge wells, with the ancient method of raising water by a long lever fixed over a tall pole.

Many carrioles stop here to change horses. We have had two Germans dining with us, who had set out for Drontheim and gone a stage on their journey, but having been driven back by the floods, turned into this, the route to the Fille Fjeld, without knowing that the same obstacles would meet them. The post, which should have passed us at Nystuen, has gone by, two days or more behind its time; the north post is many days behind, and the Swedish mail has not been heard of for more than a week. A French count and his son also call, in the same predicament as our German acquaintances; the count, quite a character, grandly commanding in a loud voice all near him, and expressing his determination to travel night and day to catch the steamer from Lierdalsoren on the night of the morrow. Even a French count, however, cannot roll back the storm, and the clouds still beat up from the south, and the rain falls furiously. Again and again travellers come and go, and we hear their news, with gloomy rumours of no steamers, and railways broken down.

Thursday morning at the smallest hours finds us awake and restless; the rain falling steadily, the wind south-west. It is a gloomy prospect.

At five we breakfast, and in an hour are each driving a quick cream-coloured pony in the direction of Gjovik, on the Mjosen Vand. The road is still through the fir plantation through which we had driven the night before last, level and uninteresting. The rain has ceased now, and a broad band of promise overspreads the western sky. Occasionally we have glimpses of the Mjosen Lake; now we dip into a sweet dell for a few minutes; then the road runs flat again, and we drive into Gjovik about eight o'clock.

It is half submerged by the floods; quite a populous place; at least a hundred or more houses and shops; evidently a new and thriving little town. We walk up the hill, after leaving our carrioles, and obtain new views of the extensive lake,—a soft, cultivated scene,—a vast Windermere. From Lillehammer, at its head, to Eidsvold, at the foot, the Mjosen Vand is nearly eighty miles long down its centre. The steamers that ply up and down, skirting its shores, and calling at some half-dozen small towns and stations on their way, make a voyage each way daily of 120 miles.

At Hamer, on the eastern shore, about midway down the lake, the effects of the great storm and floods were very marked. We had previously passed the church at Naes, surrounded with water to a depth of several feet; but here half the town was uninhabitable, except in the upper storeys of the houses. The entire length of the town was submerged to the height of the middle of the shop windows, and boats moved about from street to street and house to house, to carry the inmates away. In many places the people could only just escape wetting on the first floor.

The water was still rising; since yesterday it had gained six inches; the day before twelve inches. On the Sunday gone by, the water had begun to rise an inch and a half per hour, and continued at that rate for forty-eight hours or more. The people were fast becoming terror stricken. There had been no such flood since the year 1789, the captain of the steamer informed us; the lake was now higher by 38 feet than its ordinary level, with every probability, in case of warmer weather, which would bring down rapidly the yet unmelted snows, of a further rise. "There were, therefore," the captain said, "no travellers whatsoever, except foreigners like yourself, who will or must go on, whatever is in the way." This great increase in the elevation of the surface of the water would doubtless affect the aspect of the country, which, to us, appeared tame. The land on the shores of the Mjosen is well cultivated, and is considered of the best in Norway. There are several very large farms hereabouts, and one or two extensive breweries.

Eidsvold is prettily situated at the foot of the lake; indeed it is a few miles up the river, in ordinary times a narrow stream running out of the lake, but now all is one undistinguishable broad expanse of water. The hotel, many houses, the railway stations, and the bridges are all under water. We are taken by the steamboat as near as practicable to the mouth of the railway tunnel, and thence conveyed in small boats up the tunnel, half filled with water. Then we walk along trucks over which planks are placed for footing, and by-and-by emerge from this unsatisfactory position upon dry land, and walk along the rails to the train, about half a mile distant. It is a single line of rails; in other respects we might be at home. The engine is a Stephenson, and the carriages have an English maker's name. The officials are clothed on English models, and our tickets manufactured ditto. In the matter of speed only do we perceive a falling off, and in this we are much behind even English parliamentary trains. There is no hurry, no banging of doors, and wild screeching of the eager engine; all is done calmly and methodically. In fact, I do not remember in all the country to have seen a Norwegian in a hurry. It is an inconceivable condition.

The greater proportion of the road runs through dense pine forests, the noblest we have seen. The loftiest pines, and so thickly growing as to shut out the bright sunlight streaming from the west, and reddening the distant eastern hills with its rich glow.

In one part the rails were twelve or fifteen inches under water, for about a quarter of a mile; and the country for many miles was one vast lake. We saw several rafts and numerous boats, crowded with people and their goods. Once or twice we saw them escaping to the rafts through the roofs of the water-surrounded houses. It was a distressing sight, and filled us with melancholy.

We left Eidsvold at half-past five; and at about half-past nine we are gently descending an incline from which we look down upon the capital of Norway, beautifully placed at the head of the great Christiania Fjord. It is still bright with the glow of the setting sun as we stroll along the modern streets of this once quaint city. The great fires of recent years have cleared away most of the old timber houses, and there are now long lines of fine shops and warehouses, as in an English town. We seek the Victoria Hotel, an excellent hostelry, and after an enjoyable supper, quickly ready, wander out once more.

A Norwegian acquaintance we had made on board the *Mjosen* steamer takes us towards the palace, finely situated on the high ground, with approaching slopes that form pleasant walks for the citizens. Then we visit the Klinkenberg, the Cremorne of Christiania; and in an atmosphere of tobacco smoke, reeking with the odours of schnapps and beer, listen to a few songs, amorous and otherwise, from a company of German vocalists, the fair members of which appear to have great attractions to young Christiania, who laughingly chats to the particular fair one whose turn it is to take round the tray for the skillings each person is expected to contribute after each song.

We adjourn from this place, passing on our way the Theatre, the Bank of Norway, and several other public buildings, to the Freemasons' Hall, a similar institution to the one we have left, minus the gardens of innocence so nicely described by Mr. Williams as surrounding the Klinkenberg.

At the Freemasons' Hall, in addition to the smoke, schnapps, and love ditties of three Norwegian, German, and Swedish syrens, accompanied and conducted by a monster basso profundo, there was also the educational assistance of a large billiard table.

My own unsophisticated impression of these "innocent recreations" was, that "fast" young men are the same in Christiania as in other places; and that "women and wine" are pretty much the same now as they were in the days of Alcibiades or the patriarchs.

The next day we had only a few hours, and these were quickly gone in a ramble through the shops, picking up two or three trifles to bring away; in running down to the pleasant baths, and plunging into the open and refreshing fjord; in sauntering round the quays, where many ships are moored, and in watching the stream of life flow slowly past the window of our hotel.

The influence of general intercourse with the world has taken away from Christiania the distinguished outward characteristics of Norwegian manners and customs, and contrasts very markedly with Bergen and the western districts. There we had often remarked upon the almost Tartar type of face; and frequently observed how Eastern-like were the women's dresses and the shape of buildings. The almost sacred feelings of hospitality to strangers, too, had something Eastern in their manifestation; reminding us, in fact, in many ways of that great wave of human life which ages ago had swept over Europe from the distant East, the cradle of our race, and which in its ebb and flow had carried to the North those Gothic hordes, of which the Scandinavian family is probably the least altered modern type.

At Christiania I should recommend the Victoria as the best hotel; we met with every attention, although our appearance was decidedly "seedy;" the charges moderate, excellent fare, and pleasant company.

In the afternoon, about five, the *Scandinavian* slowly steamed out of the harbour, amidst much waving of handkerchiefs and "Farvels." The domestic and social ties are very close in Norway. I do not remember ever to have seen so quietly-demonstrative a crowd as that which waved us its adieux from Christiania. As we steamed down the fjord, the view of the receding city was most pleasing. Placed in the centre of a semicircle formed by pine-covered mountains; its buildings descending to the water's edge, crowded with the shipping of various nations; the streets rising terrace-like, with the great palace of the king prominent over all; with fine spires interspersed, and the great dome of the Cathedral Church gilled with the rays of the setting sun, in bright contrast to the deeper orange and purple tints of the distant mountains—it was a lovely picture to carry away with one's last look of the land where we had enjoyed so much that was beautiful. And when all this had passed out of sight, and the dark forms of the hills and mountains outlined themselves against the clear western sky, and the clouds hurried away and rolled themselves massively in the East, and the evening deepened into night, and the air became clearer, the distant rocky coast more strongly marked, the rich tints of sunset more glowing, and the crescent moon of that longest day in June looked faintly through the golden halo of the skies—we realized the full depth of beauty of that picture to which we had so long looked forward, of midnight on the Christiania Fjord.

We touched at Christiansand on our homeward passage. It is a very clean, quiet little fishing town, with more costume visible than in Christiania, and the houses are mostly of wood.

Again we move out, and steam across the wild North Sea; the wind is in our teeth, and by-and-by we are struggling against a gale. We have roughish work from Saturday night to Monday morning, when we sight the low shores of York and Lincoln, and by four o'clock in the afternoon cast anchor in the Humber, opposite to the massive tower of Trinity Church, Hull.

We have been away twenty-four days. Our expenses, when we reach Manchester, will have been £21 each; more than £11 each of which has been consumed in going to and from Norway. £20 was more than sufficient for both of us during our sojourn there for everything. I should say that £25 would be ample funds for a month, and would be sufficient to cover the preparatory expenses of a knapsack, map, roadbook, vocabulary, light silk waterproof cape,—in short, everything necessary for the expedition.

My outfit consisted of a suit of shepherd's plaid, lined throughout with flannel; two figured flannel shirts, three pairs of woollen socks, a change of shoes, brushes, razor, note book, map, dictionary, solid sketch book, writing materials, and a thick Scotch plaid.

It is a great saving of time, and very desirable before leaving home, to write out as complete a plan as possible of the route to be taken, in which each day's work is allotted, with an occasional day for rest.

It has now been demonstrated that, even for men engaged in close attention to business, which in Manchester, where gold is God, and where work is consequently carried on at a higher pressure than elsewhere, a visit to grand old Norway is quite practicable, and, with a little preparation, easy ; and I am disposed to think at a less average expense than to any other country, or, with the same continuous movement, in any part of our own attractive land.

Should the appearance of these very imperfect sketches, written entirely during our excursion, become the means of inducing others to go and do something of the kind, and so in a certain remote way help to bind together, by increased intercourse, two nations so intimately connected by descent, it will be one more lasting source of satisfaction to the writer and his comrade, connected with their Three Weeks' Ramble in Norway.

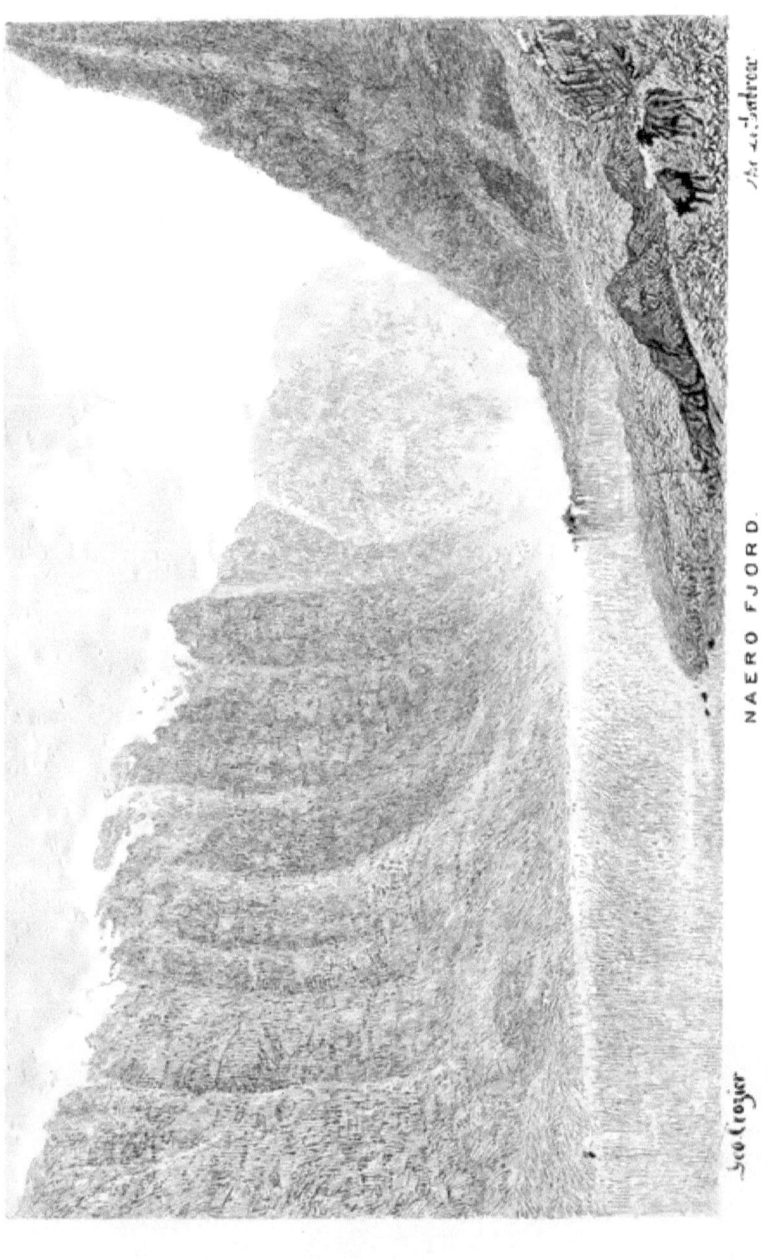

NAERO FJORD.

www.ingramcontent.com/pod-product-compliance
Lightning Source LLC
Chambersburg PA
CBHW030244170426
43202CB00009B/617